From the Heart

(a collection of
very short stories)

Erik Smith

HURON
RIVER
PRESS

ISBN: 1-932399-12-7

Huron River Press
201 South Main Street
Suite 900
HURON   Ann Arbor, MI 48104
RIVER   www.huronriverpress.com
PRESS

Library of Congress Cataloging-in-Publication Data
Smith, Erik, 1943-
  From the heart : (a collection of very short stories) / Erik Smith.
     p. cm.
  ISBN 1-932399-12-7
  1. Michigan--Biography--Anecdotes. 2. Michigan--Social life and customs--Anecdotes. I. Title.
  CT241.S65 2006
  977.4--dc22
                        2006006574

Printed in the United States of America.

For "Lonestar" Charley

The mind reels...

Contents

Preface

The stories found on the following pages have their roots firmly in the soil of daily life in Michigan. They are, for the most part, simple tales about people just like us. In fact, they are about all of us who have dreams, and about the exceptional few who have actually dared to live them.

The stories span the transition into a new century and a new millennium, yet they are virtually timeless. They are testimony to the human spirit, to the American way of life, and to the overwhelming evidence of goodwill we so often fail to recognize as we rocket along in the high-speed lanes of modern life.

This book began as a bold experiment in local television. Amid the chaos, bloodshed, and political debauchery of what usually defines the "news" of the day, the Scripps-Howard broadcasting stations were challenged to strike a more realistic balance in their daily programs.

What better way to achieve that balance than to look into the lives of individuals who would probably never make the nightly news or even the feature page of their local newspaper.

Thus, *From the Heart* was born.

Acknowledgments

I wish to recognize my beloved life's companion and wife, Sharon Smith, for her encouragement and support in the preparation and publication of this story collection.

Special tribute goes to WXYZ-TV producer Sandy McPhee and videographer Bob Berg who turned my simple words into something truly unique in local television's vast wasteland. They made it work!

Thanks to my many mentors, teachers, and heroes whose names could fill another book. Thanks to the National Academy of Television Arts and Sciences. The National Association of Producers and Television Executives, The Radio and Television News Directors Association, the management of Scripps-Howard Broadcasting, the Michigan Associated Press Broadcaster's Association, Wayne State University, and to each of you who read this book for recognizing what quality television has to offer us.

Finally, my gratitude and love to my TV bosses, Grace Gilchrist, Marla Drutz and Andrea Parquet-Taylor for their unwavering faith and confidence in my work.

Erik Smith

April 2006

Childhood

The Faces in the Calendar

What is it that we see when we look into the face of a child? What is there that brings us such joy, such reassurance, such unconditional love, or in some cases, such burdening pain?

Perhaps we really see ourselves in a living mirror, an image that offers us a fleeting glance at what we once were. Perhaps we see the time when life was measured without boundaries, when emotions flowed without the restraint of inhibitions, when we were able to sleep in our beds without cares.

Kendra Dew has spent her life as a grownup looking directly into those living mirrors. Through a lens and view-finder, she searches for those instants, those mini-moments measured only in children's time.

"I always loved to photograph children," the artist explains. "I had a little camera as a kid, and ran around taking pictures of all my friends. I guess I was born to it. It's just something I've always wanted to do." Kendra is not much for sitting still. If one drops by her studio in Berkeley, Michigan, she'll be somewhere near a camera or the photo painting room. Chances are she'll be working on a project that she began a few years ago. It's an annual calendar featuring the innocent faces of childhood. Twelve angelic portraits, each painstakingly hand-tinted, not to obscure their place and time, but to celebrate the truths of Down syndrome.

"We want these children to be seen just like any other child is photographed," Kendra says as she stops for a moment in the small room with the Victorian chairs that serves as a waiting area to her studio a few steps away. "Sure, these kids may have special needs, but they are photographed just like any other child in a childlike setting."

The annual calendar is the passion of Cynthia Kidder. She is a teacher, dedicated mother, and now tireless crusader. Cynthia's heart was strained years ago when her son, Jordan, was born with the extra chromosome responsible for Down syndrome. At the time, doctors couldn't tell her much; medically far less was known at the time about the syndrome. Now, however, Cynthia has the facts, and she is busy spreading them with the evangelical fervor of a strengthened heart.

"The emotional reward for me comes from the parents. I got a call from a new father on his cell phone. He was confused and distraught about his child, so he called me from his car. A nurse at the hospital had given him one of our calendars and he wanted to talk, to say thanks. He said, 'My little girl can be beautiful'…and that's what the calendar is all about." It was proof to Cynthia of her mission's purpose.

The calendar of twelve is the centerpiece in the alliance of love. But Cynthia and Kendra are working on other ideas too. Other ideas to spread the good news about Down syndrome. Greeting cards are now being added to the inventory of the company Cynthia has started called "Band of Angels." All of the cards feature the timeless portraitures of Kendra Dew. The venture is literally a labor of love. It hasn't turned a dime of profit, but that's not the point, is it?

Cynthia sums it up in a couple of sentences. "Our kids are so much like any other kids are. They're curious, rambunctious; they need love and attention." Cynthia Kidder's passionate mission comes easily in just a few additional words. "The earlier you can communicate the facts to the parents is so important. We have to teach them to believe in their child."

As another year in the crusade passes, there will be a new calendar, probably in a Hallmark store at the nearest mall or neighborhood shopping center.

The tinted Victorian images will gaze back at us with the same unspoken joy, love, and innocence, but perhaps with a better understanding than we once had. Together, we are now able to look into that special mirror that the children of Down syndrome are holding up for us to see.

A Place to Read

The silencing shroud of another winter greets first the eye and the ear. The greens have gone brown, and the sounds of a summer past linger only in the mind or perhaps somewhere out there in the frozen reeds of the St. John's marsh.

We have come to the island in winter, Harsen's Island, a summer playground at the edge of Anchor Bay where in winter, only the very determined choose to stay. The days are short and the nights long, linked to the mainland only by a ferry that adheres to a schedule largely determined by the caprices of Mother Nature.

Time doesn't stand still here, but it does hang heavy in the hands of the young. There are no shopping malls, no movie houses, no burger joints, just school and life on a remote island street to occupy the times of day.

"He was awakened early the next morning by a thundering crash. What was it, he thought as he sprang to his feet in the middle of the empty room." The words fall softly from the adult woman in the bulky sweater who carefully balances

7

the oversized book on her lap. In a haphazard semicircle surrounding her, about a dozen elementary-school-age children sit transfixed as the story unfolds.

It is late on a Tuesday afternoon. The school day is finished, and the ever-present clouds of December are masking the remains of the daylight that fades beyond the frosted plate glass window. The children of Harsen's Island are listening to the words from a book, each page coming alive from the donated volume that has become a favorite selection of the young readers-to-be.

Scarcely a year ago, none of this existed. There were no books; there were no shelves to hold the books. There was no carpet on the floor. There were no chairs and no place to sit. There was only a boarded-up vacant storefront and an idea without a name.

"It had been abandoned and boarded up for over ten years," says Barb Persyn, a longtime island resident. "We looked at it and said, what are we gonna do? How can we make this work?"

A neighbor, Sue Masters, is eager to answer the question. "Luckily, one of the other neighbors came by when we were looking at this place and asked us how he could help. He happens to own a glass company on the mainland. Well, two weeks later, here he comes and suddenly there's a new picture window being put in. We ask him, how much? He says 'Nothing, glad to help. We need a library for the kids.'" And that is how it really began.

Perhaps it's the kind of thing that can only happen on an island where fifteen hundred people live, but let's hope not. The parents and kids all wanted a library. They wanted a place to meet, a place to read, a place to teach, a place for residents to feel a sense of community. So they decided to make it happen.

"Everything you see here," Barb gestures proudly, "everything here is volunteered. The books, the furniture, the computer, everything was donated to us. The churches helped out. Some of the books came from a library on the mainland that had some extras or doubles. It's just unbelievable when you think about it."

There is no brass plaque on the wall to honor the citizens who brought The Reader's Cove to life. They know who they are. The furnace man, the window man, the husband, the wife, the retiree who lives over on the south channel, the teacher, the bar owner, the guy down the street who always has the nativity scene out on the front lawn at the start of the holiday season. They all pooled their individual talents, made the most of their limited resources, and built a special place from the bottom of their hearts.

Sue Masters gets a little emotional about it all. With a halting determination in her voice she says, "Honestly, I feel a little ethereal about it…sometimes, I have to pinch myself to believe what we've all been able to do. I really believe it was just meant to be."

Their dream of an island library is still in the making. There is a big space in the rear of the storefront building that's still in need of a lot of work. The bathrooms are on the future wish list, and we should hope the future can be hurried up on that end. There is an abiding confidence these days in The Reader's Cove, that the improvements will continue to come. They will come, as surely as another summer, when the sun-seekers and the boaters return once again to the haven of Harsen's Island.

And when the people of the summer do return, they'll probably drop by to visit The Reader's Cove, where their children will read or listen to a favorite book while school is in recess for the warm days of a Michigan year. All too quickly, however, the leaves will begin to turn colors, the boats will hide beneath their canvas covers, and the silent shroud of winter will cloak the marshes once again.

The summer people will be gone, but when the first snows blanket the empty street across from the Sans Souci Bar, there will be a welcoming light in the window behind the frosted glass. There will be a door to open, a place to sit, a book to read, a conversation to join, and a spirit alive in the community called The Reader's Cove.

Blackwater Surprise

It's hard to put a label on it. It's not rap music, but it is. It's not rock or soul, but it is. It's not the blues or country music, but it is. It is Detroit music in a new century. A new—yet old—sound that's gritty, bucket-bottomed, and simply irresistible to a growing legion of fans. It is the music of Robert Bradley's Blackwater Surprise. It is music for the street, born in the street, and to be danced in the street.

The sound is achieved through an unlikely blending of diversity. Four young, white, once-upon-a-time rock-and-rollers, and a slightly over-fifty blind, black poet and street singer have come together in a strange coalition and coalescence of styles. Oddly enough, the first notes came on a breeze from an open window on a busy corner near Woodward and Michigan Avenue.

"I came running up here and told the guys," Jeff Fowlkes recalls with vivid detail. "You gotta hear this, man...So we all run to the window, pop it open, and listen. It was like, wow, has this guy got a set of pipes, or what?" The voice they heard belonged to Robert Bradley, wafting through the autumn air like the burnished leaves that were dropping from the locust trees in the busy city park below.

While their meeting was by chance, there is a rock-and-roll fairy tale quality to it. The band boys quickly rushed into the streets to find the singer and whisked him up into the loft that houses their fairly sophisticated recording studio. For hours, the white boys and their new street friend made music together.

"It was like crazy, man. We just played and played, picking up on Robert's grooves and adding some little licks of our own here and there. We recorded everything and when RCA heard it, they were blown away. We just rolled the tape, no rehearsal." Mike Nehra describes the musical melding with the kind of enthusiasm one might expect to hear from the miner who found the Hope diamond.

Okay, it's not a fairy tale, but it certainly is a promoter's dream. There is, however, much more to the story than just a chance encounter between a street singer and a bunch of rocking guitar slingers. Maybe the magic didn't really happen overnight, but it did begin the way they said it did.

Robert Bradley had more than a little skepticism to overcome. He was happy enough just to be picking up a few bucks a day singing on his favorite sweet street corner. "Sweet" because, he says, he could hear himself in stereo between the polished building walls in the belly of the city. Robert Bradley never sold pencils or panhandled his way along those streets. He came most days with his guitar to sing and entertain and give voice to the words and music that constantly were swirling around in his head. His music was his survival chord.

Robert's musical philosophy of the street is not complex. "If you get to the right place, if you can find that echo, that's the place, man. That's where you wanna be...to hear that echo, man. You hear that, and you don't have to sing as strong to be heard, you know what I mean?" This is Robert's simple explanation of the complex search for acoustic perfection.

It took some time for the Blackwater Surprise to really happen. After all, they were forging a new musical sound from Motown. It was to become a self-produced, self-titled album that would eventually propel them into a big-label deal with RCA and ultimately onto the video charts of MTV. One of the band's songs, called "Trouble Brother," even found its way into a movie soundtrack for the film *The Devil's Own* starring Brad Pitt and Harrison Ford. Now that's getting pretty close to fairy-tale stuff!

These days, Robert's Blackwater Surprise is spending a lot of time on the road. They're basically playing one-nighters in clubs and small concert halls to support not only sales of their record, but to meet and make new fans, and to enjoy the few perks that accompany the otherwise complicated trappings of success in the music business. It's hard work, but somebody's gotta do it.

For Robert Bradley it's a head-spinner. He says he's just the blind man who wants to put his music of Detroit front and center again. The long journey from Pershing High School, to that corner in Eastern Market with the special echo, to a place on *Billboard*'s list of pop hits, has been both rewarding and confounding. Life just isn't simple anymore and he's not so sure he likes it that way.

"I've had this dream since I was nine years old. I wanted to make my music. I wanted people to hear it. Yeah, it took me a little while, but you know, I never did give up." He says it with candor and the wrinkled smile that seems to cross those countenances which have borne the weight of maturity, and in his case, disabilities.

It's not a real rags-to-riches story yet, but Robert Bradley certainly doesn't have to carry a tin cup with him anymore. His days of riding the hound are clearly over too. He recently completed a series of haunting television commercials for The Henry Ford Museum in Dearborn, and his battered old guitar has been replaced with an instrument that reflects his new stature in the business of music.

No one can guess where the road will eventually take the boys of Blackwater Surprise, but you can bet that a blind man will show them the way.

Mr. A.

The voice booms across the cement floor, bounces off the scarred walls, reflects over the hood of a vintage automobile, and finally comes to rest in the ears of a group of high-school kids who have just arrived to begin another day.

"All right, I want to see some productivity around here today. Grab those paper towels, the torches are over there on the press...okay, are we listening, let's go, let's go."

The voice belongs to Frank Antonucci. The kids just call him "Mr. A." Welcome to first hour, Auto Body One, at the Career Prep Center in Macomb County. For a motorhead, this is as close to heaven as it ever gets. The air reeks with the scent of fresh paint, Bondo, and sweat.

"This is a Z-28 with the hideaway headlamps," Mr. A explains to a visitor. "It belongs to that beauty on the hoist over there." On the hoist is something that looks like it was recently pardoned from the local junkyard without the dog.

For more years than he probably wants to count, Frank Antonucci has called this place home. It is the place where

15

he serves as teacher, mentor, and even friend to a lot of kids who have been short-changed on all three.

"Gimme a toothpick, we'll put a dab of glue on this one and hook it back up," he loudly explains to one of the students who looks a bit confused by the command. "Okay, now double check everything. Make sure those paint guns are secured and put away."

To the casual observer, it's organized chaos. But under Mr. A's keen eye, it gets done, and done well.

"I want these kids to be mentored, like I was mentored, like you were mentored," he says earnestly. "I was mentored with a boot up my backside. When they leave here, they'll remember that and be able to pass it on to the next generation."

Frank Antonucci is the General Patton of his young army of painters and polishers. The task is simple and complex at the same time. Take the old and make it new. Take the rusty and make it shine again. It is the auto body repair business for real, up close and personal, and done to perfection by imperfect and often impatient high-school hands.

Striking a gaze at the stripped shell of the Chevy Z-28 that perches eight feet in the air on the school's hoist, one has to wonder what kind of miracle it will take to get this derelict vehicle in show condition shape in just eleven calendar days. Not school days, calendar days.

"That's the plan," Mr. A says confidently. "I'm very confident we're gonna make the show."

On this day, there is an extra crunch on. They want to prepare not one, but two cars for the annual Autorama Show at Cobo Center in downtown Detroit. Mr. A's kids usually cop a trophy or two there every year, but last year, they blew it.

"If you had been in this classroom last year at this same time, it was all disassembled like this car on the rack and we almost had it, but the details were lacking." Mr. A was not happy about that.

It won't happen again, and it didn't. Eleven days later, the Z-28 was a blue metallic shining show car, standing under the spotlights behind the velvet ropes. As students beamed with obvious pride nearby, the Chevy was front and center in the Cobo Hall display area.

In a day and age when technology seems to threaten the disciplined artistry of skilled hands and minds, Auto Body One might be considered an anachronism—until one meets the young adults who are paying the rent and putting food on the table each month, thanks to the skills they have learned in Mr. A's workshop classroom over the years.

"I came in here and I didn't know what it was all about," one former student explains. "Yeah, Mr. A and I went around a few times my first year in here. You know, I was young. I had an attitude problem, so he kinda had to help straighten me out" (Mr. A doesn't deal very well with attitude).

Another former student is quick to chime in. "Mr. A teaches you a lot more than just working on cars, you know. Like he teaches you to be on time, to give it all you've got all the time so you can really feel proud of what you've done."

Soon the bell will ring and another school day will end at the Career Prep Center. There will be many dirty hands, some gray primer under the fingernails, some Bondo dust will cling to the shoulder-length hair. It's another day in the shop for a bunch of kids who don't get straight As in English or trigonometry.

But the next time a shopping cart dings your passenger side door, or you happen to back into that light pole at the dentist's office, who you gonna call? Chances are it might be one of Mr. A's kids!

"I want them to look back and say, 'Man, I wish I was back in Mr. A's class in high school, even if he was a little loud. At least I learned something from him.' I want to go down, when I do go down, with them remembering that at least they had one guy who cared about them."

Note: Frank Antonucci was severely injured in an automobile accident on his way home from a day of teaching in the auto body shop. He sustained closed head injuries when his head went through the rear window of his El Camino truck. After months and months of extensive therapy, he returned to work as the assistant principal of Warren's Cousino High School. As of this writing, he is once again back at his beloved Career Prep Center where he now serves as the school principal. No one can ever doubt Mr. A's commitment to his special kids.

Hogs on the Run

It might as well be a scene out of one of those late-night "B" movies. A gaggle of growling Harley-Davidsons thundering in unison down a stretch of endless highway. It's a rolling tableau in black leather, sparkling chrome, and iridescent paint. On any other day, it might be mistaken as a threat to the peace, a threat to law and order, and a threat to the daughters of good fathers everywhere. But hold on a second.

Wrong plot, wrong movie, wrong stereotypes. You see, that is a police escort up front. Okay, the bikers have commandeered the road, but they are on their way to bring some smiles, some cheer, but more importantly, some personal time to warm the hearts of a lot of kids at Detroit's Children's Hospital.

"It's a simple thing, really" says the man with the shaved head that reflects in the shiny burgundy paint on his Harley's gas tank. "It's all about putting a smile on one kid's face for just one hour." His name is Kaz Mamon.

When Kaz puts out the word each year that it's time to fire up and ride for the kids, it's not unusual to have a thousand bikes show up. What is unusual is the fact that Kaz asks each of them to pay to ride along with him, and pay they do. The riders of the roaring hogs kick in thousands of dollars to help sick kids continue their education while they are hospitalized, often for extended periods of time. It's Mamon's annual mission, and he makes the most of it.

"It's just a great feeling to know that you can bring some happiness to a kid. That you can give an hour of your time and help brighten up a day and help a kid stay up with some schoolwork that he's missing out on while he's in the hospital." Those are the words that come from the feeling in Kaz's heart.

You might guess that Kaz is one of those people who doesn't take "No" for an answer very well. The words *it can't be done* are just not part of his vocabulary. Neither is the word *impossible*—and because of that, a lot of money has been raised and some very sick children have been made to feel a lot better, at least for a while.

Modesty seems to fit well on the frame of this physically big man. He's always the first to point out, "It's not just one person who gets this done. It takes everybody to make it work. From the cops, the clubs, the hospital staff and volunteers…it's just everybody pitchin' in for the kids."

Good ideas seem to have a way of taking on a life of their own. Kaz Mamon's idea to help educate hospitalized kids struck a lot of sensitive nerves in the biker community around Detroit a few years back. Now, each time he plans a ride, he get a lot of motors running, both figuratively and literally.

For example, he had this idea about computers. Why not get some computers in the hands of the kids in the hospital? They've got too much time on their hands during treatment anyway, so why not put computers into those hands? Kaz put the idea in motion. Soon, he was on the phone to some corporate folks, and before long, there was a truckload of used laptops arriving at his back door.

In so many ways, Kaz is the embodiment of the mythical gentle giant. I don't know what he weighs, but there's at least six feet and a few inches of him between his shoes and his hairline. He lives alone in the sprawling house that he built with his own two hands, listening to Mozart in stereo, or polishing up the many crystal figurines he has collected and displayed so proudly around his home. His home is his castle, but the truth is, he's not here very much these days.

Kaz also happens to own his own trucking business and as if that weren't enough to keep him busy, he also works the night shift at G.M.'s Lake Orion Assembly Plant. You get the feeling his average day must be about twenty-eight hours long. All of this, and somehow he finds the time to care for other people's kids in crisis. So, how does he do it?

"I just do it," he answers simply. "Look, it's a great feeling to know that I'm just one guy who can get a thousand people to come together and make some kids feel good." Then he gets to the heart of the matter. "You know, one person comes out, sees what it's about. He tells another person, who tells another person, and then you've got something rolling. It's about the kids, man."

Let's just say the story of Kaz Mamon's annual ride for children is really an "A" movie. After all, it has a solid plot, some very interesting characters, a lot of unusual special effects, and it's rated "G" for general audiences everywhere. It's particularly well suited for young children, wouldn't you agree?

A Teacher's Teacher

It is two or three hours before the school bell is scheduled to ring and proclaim the start of another day in the class-room. Seated behind a large glass window that looks into the cavernous hallway beyond, Ray Lawson is back at his desk where he has been a fixture since 1946. The desk and room have changed over the years, but the mission has not. The computer in front of him hadn't been invented when Mr. Lawson started teaching high-school English over fifty-five years ago.

When others much younger than he is count the days until their retirement, Ray Lawson, like the river in the Gershwin song, just keeps rollin' along.

"I think of every year as a new challenge," says the iron man of English education. "I throw away all of my lesson plans from the previous year and take a look at the new students and try to decide just what they will need in the months ahead."

Mr. Lawson, as his students reverently call him, is some-thing of a legend in the Rochester, Michigan public school system. In almost ten thousand days in the classroom, he has never appeared without a suit and tie. It's a Lawson trademark, part of teaching the Lawson way.

By some standards, his classroom methods have always been a little on the nontraditional side. He's not exactly avant-garde but he's not exactly old-school stuffy either. He's not big on tests, for example. He often asks students to grade themselves, but reserves the final word on that to himself. His classes are not free form, nor are they rigid. He likes and encourages ideas, questions, and open and frank discussions. In more than eighty years of living, Ray Lawson knows that all of life is not printed on the pages of a textbook.

"I have a strange way of teaching writing, for instance. I tell them to say it first, and then smooth it out a little on paper. I feel I can be on their level and we can talk...we can talk about anything." That's the Lawson approach to education in the classroom.

A typical school day for the octogenarian educator begins about 5:00 A.M. when he arrives at the building. He likes the quiet time, maybe ninety minutes or so, before the students begin to trickle in to talk with him. It is his time to prepare for the five straight teaching hours on his feet that await him every day. There is a break or two in the routine, but then he also must face a number of English department chores, a couple of personal conferences with kids or parents, then sometime after 5:00 P.M., it's time to go home. Kind of your typical twelve-hour day when teaching children happens to be your chosen profession.

"Quite often, I'll put my lesson plan on the back burner and just open the floor for discussion on a particular subject. We've tackled some pretty interesting topics over the years.

You know, these young people face some very challenging things in their lives and talking about them together helps all of them."

It goes without saying in his fifty-plus years in the classroom that Ray Lawson has influenced a lot of lives. His students have become successful doctors, lawyers, business folks, teachers, and even an auto mechanic or two.

He has taught the children of his first students. Then he taught their children, and now he's teaching the children of their children. By his guesstimate, he has seen well over nineteen thousand children in his class, enough of them to fill most of the seats in Joe Louis Arena.

Not long ago, many of Ray Lawson's kids gathered to pay tribute and honor the man who personified the word *education* to them. There were speeches, and many memories recalled during the evening. Ray was gratified, of course, but slightly uncomfortable with the recognition of his job well done. He is a very modest man, as any of his students will be quick to tell you.

By every measure, the gathering of graduates was a smashing success. Over thirty thousand dollars was raised in Ray's honor to establish a teacher education fund that will bear his name for future generations to remember. For the man in the perfectly pressed suit and matching tie, it was all about another day's work.

"So long as I feel good, I'll keep at it," he says in his quiet voice that obviously doesn't wish to verbalize the word *retirement*.

"If I wake up on some Wednesday morning and think, my gosh, it's only Wednesday and I've got three more days to go...well, then I'll know it's time to quit."

A lot has certainly changed in Ray Lawson's long life. He has watched the Rochester area grow and sprawl from a small rural village into a bulging and prosperous suburb. He has watched as lined paper theme books have morphed into laptop computer screens, and handwriting has all but been surrendered to a keyboard and a thing called a mouse. But the challenge of teaching hasn't changed in all of his years, and that is what keeps calling him back to class every September.

"It's still fun for me. You see, I believe we have to laugh. We have to laugh every day because when we laugh, we truly see ourselves." It is Ray Lawson's personal philosophy of living and he has put his heart in it, and managed to keep it there far longer than most of us.

Note: Ray Lawson retired after the 2003-04 school year.

A Quilt for Baby Doe

The ideas slipped right through the eye of a needle. After all, she had been sewing since her childhood days, so it was only natural that a housewife from Waterford Township would take a needle, some thread, and some scraps of cloth to fashion what would become the first of hundreds of quilts for tiny babies.

Ellen Ann knew something about babies. Her son, Mitchell, had been born prematurely. The stark, sterile atmosphere of the hospital infirmary made a lasting impression on the new mother. As she gazed into the nursery, she vowed to do something for all the little ones she saw in those bubble-topped incubators. She wanted to do something that would welcome those new lives into a new world and comfort them at the same time.

"It hit me as I was looking around at all those babies in there," Ellen Ann explains. "Those tiny legs and arms needed to be covered. I just think they needed to be warm...and I thought about a quilt." Ellen looks very much like everybody's first-grade teacher, so when she talks, one has the tendency to listen. "They're so small when they're starting out in life, and I thought a quilt might keep them healthy and make a keepsake for the moms who are just waiting for that child to be able to come home." Ellen knows the feeling. She glances at her son Mitchell who is playing on the floor, a few feet away in the dining room.

It was just a simple little idea. It did, however, come directly from Ellen Ann's heart, so it shouldn't be a surprise that her little idea gained momentum around the country, and the Tiny Miracles Project was soon born. It was little more than an idea to bring little quilts to little babies who had chosen to arrive just a little too early.

"Just yesterday, I received this wonderful note from a new mother who had one of our quilts wrapped around her baby," Ellen says proudly. "I get phone calls, e-mails, letters, cards, and they are all so wonderful and warm. These are from total strangers…it's wonderful."

In Michigan, about 23,000 babies are born prematurely each year. That's a lot of quilts to make by any standard, so demand may always outstrip Ellen's abilities to supply. At least these days, she has some help. Some good friends, a few neighbors, and a couple of folks far away have become Ellen's sewing sisters in the Tiny Miracles crusade.

"Really, it has taken off," Ellen says as she looks over a fresh bolt of cloth. "You see all this material?" Her hand gestures in a wide sweep that stretches for a yard. "People from all over the country are sending me cloth for the quilts. That used to be the biggest concern I had: where to find all the cloth I needed. Now it just seems to come to me when I need it."

Ellen doesn't have what most women would call a sewing room in her house. Her entire downstairs resembles a small New England textile plant, complete with some state-of-the-art quilt-making machinery that makes her labor of the heart a little less labor-intensive. In one corner of the plant sits the sign of these times, a Dell computer displaying her Tiny Miracles site on the World Wide Web. All of this has sprung from a little idea for little people.

The payoff for all the hard work comes once a month when Ellen and her sewing sisters head for the local hospitals. Loaded down with wicker laundry baskets, they could be the washerwomen of another century, but the contents of their baskets betray them. They carry dreams full of colorful little quilts to the neo-natal intensive care units. This is the moment when all the hours, all of the work is suddenly worth it all. This is the moment of tiny miracles.

The nurse's and the quilter's hands are soon busy in the baskets. For a time, there is the temptation to match pattern to babies. For a time, there is the temptation to match colors to genders. Suddenly, neither of the procedures is deemed worthwhile, and soon tiny quilts are randomly united with tiny owners in a crazy-quilt of pattern and color. It is a scene pregnant with smiles.

Just outside the nursery, a new mother is preparing to take her newest arrival home. She has wrapped the child in a bluish quilt that arrived at the hospital only a few minutes before. It's a Kodak moment without the flash or the film.

"He's my tiny miracle," the mother explains to Ellen Ann and a nurse who has assisted her with the transition. "He's so beautiful and the quilt is so perfect. I'm going to keep it forever. It's an heirloom—the first heirloom for my baby. I just want to take him home, now…thank you so much…"

The moment passes to be recalled when, once again, the sisterhood of the seamstresses gathers.

From yards of donated cloth, from dedicated hours passed in caring hands, from mothers to mothers, and others to others, tiny miracles happen...bringing a little old-fashioned comfort to the littlest arrivals in a brand-new, high-tech world.

It's enough to warm the heart, isn't it?

A Dog Named Parker

If one were to count up all the hours that Parker the dog has spent in school, the dog would have a Ph.D. behind his name. At the very least, he should have his Master's. Oh, he does have a degree, in addition to his original pedigree. Parker is an official elementary-school counselor. He's a T.D.; that's academic lingo for therapy dog.

Parker is a co-counselor with Deb Nicholas. She is the taller member of the dynamic duo and walks on two legs. The six legs comprise the complete set of the school counseling team, whose job it is to help a lot of little kids work through some of their problems.

"Sure, you can give him the treat," Deb assures a not-so-sure first-grader. The child and the dog exchange knowing glances, and Parker consumes the first of many edible rewards which will come his way today.

Now, before jumping to any conclusions about any of this, rest assured Parker does not collect a taxpayer-funded paycheck for his daily work. That is not to say, however, that an occasional bone is not tossed his way. This is America, after all.

But Parker's not in this to beg what he can get out of it. He walks the halls and visits the classroom with a higher purpose. His job is to win the hearts and minds of the little people who reach to pat his head or stroke his back on his daily rounds as a certified therapy dog. That's his real reward, and Deb's connection to the troubles of a child.

"I think the real secret is the fact that Parker doesn't judge."

These are the words of a co-worker who has been known to sleep with the dog who quietly sits at her side. "Parker is non judgmental; he just loves everyone he comes in contact with, and hopefully, they return that same love."

While Parker's classroom visits can often resemble show and tell days, they are actually anything but. Deb and Parker are pioneering a new discipline known as "animal facilitated counseling." Those are heady words for the simple process of connecting. Its sole purpose is to connect to children's hearts and minds with the aid of a cold nose and warm, loving eyes.

In a small office that serves both Deb and dog, Parker rests on the floor next to a boy in a red sweater. The child's small right hand gently runs across the area between Parker's ears as he talks. He talks, not to Deb, but to Parker. His words flow freely, and uninhibited.

"You know, Parker seems to understand me," the boy says sincerely and softly. "He can tell when I need him." In a matter of seconds the purpose, the process, and the Parker connection are crystallized. "Parker is my friend." All questions are now answered; all doubts dispelled.

For his part, Parker puts a lot of miles on his four paws each week. On this Tuesday, he's meeting friends at Southwest Elementary School in Howell, Michigan. Tomorrow, he's off to Voyager Elementary School across town. There's not much time off during the school year, and Parker even has a schedule for the weekends at Children's Hospital in downtown Detroit. He even has his own I.D. badge there to get by security. There are a lot of kids who need his special kind of help.

"He's particularly effective with a child who has lost a close family member," Deb explains, not so much as a pioneer, but as a partner who has seen something amazing work over and over again. "A bond is established almost immediately between Parker and child. Before long the child is opening up, talking about the pain of the loss."

Parker has come a long way since Deb picked him out of a litter in Williamston. He has put on some weight and learned his manners well. The business of learning to tie his shoes doesn't apply in his case, so he has matured without complications. Deb says his heart is always in his work, and usually worn on one of his front legs.

"He can go into a classroom and immediately go directly to the child that needs him." The counselor-keeper seems almost astonished and surprised by her partner's sensibilities. "I don't know how he knows; he just knows, that's all. In a roomful of kids, he will always find the one that needs him right then."

On this day in October, Parker and Deb have a pretty busy year in front of them. Come summer, however, things do calm down a bit. Yes, Parker actually takes some time off. Deb says he really enjoys a nap in the summer sun and he likes to go on picnics in one of the Metroparks. Just like his special kids, Parker also loves to go swimming in the lake by Deb's house. That's where Parker really gets away from it all, chasing sticks and the Canada geese that taunt him down along the shoreline.

"He's a lot more than just a dog to the kids," Deb says in the confidence that comes with watching something worthy unfold. "He's an example that can make a difference in their lives. We want them to know they can make a difference too."

Digitally Divided

We used to call it the generation gap: that strange, rather opaque distance that stretched between the years of youth and the onset of acquired maturity. It is a never-never land of taste, style, and language which seems to separate children from their parents, and parents from their parents.

In the techno-age, the generation gap has come to be known as the digital divide. While it is not restricted solely to age in this modern incarnation, the divide does seem to clearly delineate those who are techno-savvy from those of us who are techno-terrified. I place myself in the latter category.

Frankly, it's been a long while since I thought a ten-year-old had much to say that I needed to hear; maybe that's a throwback to the old generation-gap thing. However, at the Long Elementary School in Dearborn, Michigan, many of us who have been digitally divided are now listening to ten-year-old teachers because the kids are as knowledgeable about computers and the darned Internet as some of us are about the A.A.R.P.

"Okay kids, here come the antiques!" shouts one of the senior citizens who has just stepped off the bus that has brought them to the school. Within minutes, the group shuffles along the locker-lined hallway for another session of elementary-school Computer Education 101.

This novel learning experience bridging the digital divide is the brainstorm of teacher Deanne Jones. She wanted to expand the school's horizons in the community, so she decided to try to hook up the Pepsi Generation with the Geritol set in front of a monitor and a mouse...and it worked.

"The kids are so excited to see the seniors come in each week," Deanne says. "The kids are so good and the seniors are so nice. They all feel a closeness to each other."

Every Tuesday at one o'clock in the afternoon, the over-eighty gang from the Oakwood Retirement Center arrive in the computer lab for their day in school. It doesn't take long before each computer is humming and e-mails fly away to loved ones in another state or country. Now, each Tuesday afternoon, every little teacher has a teacher's pet for the day.

Deanne is quick to explain, "We've managed to hook up each of the seniors with their own e-mail address, so each week they come in to read their mail and send a letter. It's surprising how quickly they pick up just what the students are showing them."

It is remarkable when one considers that almost seventy years of living span the distance between the hands that move across the keyboard. To be sure, some of the mature students in this class probably haven't typed a word since leaving high school fifty years ago. No matter—hunt and peck is still a working methodology in this gentle subtraction of the digital divide. Time really separates no one in this room for at least an hour. For sixty minutes every Tuesday, everyone in the computer lab at Long Elementary School is just ten years old.

"You know, we hear an awful lot of stories, negative stories about kids these days," Deanne says. "But I think we're proving that every age group has something to offer us, young or old."

When the school year ends in June, some of the senior students say they'll be getting computers of their own. They like this Internet thing, they say. Some have already taken pictures of their junior teachers home and taped them to the refrigerator door. In a way, they tell me, they have acquired a new grandchild to share with their friends.

I guess you could say it's a mega-byte idea that has seemed to click in everyone's heart.

Two Hearts in Gold Creek

It wears its nickname well, this place called Montana. It is the Big Sky Country where there is room to breathe, room to listen to a cascading mountain stream, a place to hear only the cheery call of a meadowlark perched in the distant pines.

There is no drone of a city's wheels, no relentless hum of our society's fixation with the excesses of technology. There is only the wind to mask the silence that envelops the soul and seems to command a moment of personal reflection at every turn.

It is vast, yet somehow confining to a flatlander. It is home to some 900,000 people, yet they are fairly hard to find when one looks about. Highway 90 winds west from the airport at Missoula and will carry us to our destination on this summer's day. The rental car odometer will spin over fifty times before we turn off the highway at Gold Creek, the very name bearing witness to its own history.

On a sloping hillside, nestled in the foothills of the Rocky Mountains, we have come to Camp Mak-A-Dream. As the car proceeds up the meandering road, children play in the field in front of the timber cabins that dot the green landscape. The air is punctuated by the sounds of fun. The shrieks of youth ring in the air as an orange disc flies from hand to hand among the players in the grass.

It is clear from the beginning that this is not the summer camp where the idle rich annually place their children each summer. Nor is it the sanctuary where countless urban well wishers send the underprivileged for a taste of life beyond the perimeters of concrete and asphalt. This is, rather, a place for a special few. A place for a fraternity of children who together face a dreaded challenge: cancer.

They come from everywhere to this place, to this hillside, to the big lodge, to their scattered cabins. They come to gather under the big Montana skies to be together, to share their individual battle stories, their fears, and their personal experiences. They come to Camp Mak-A-Dream for a week to be children, not patients or victims. This week they will not be alone with their hopes, dreams, and fears.

"They leave their baggage at the door," says Doctor Stu, one of the camp's many volunteers who make the pilgrimage to this mountainside to be with the children. "They are accepted for who they are and they are never alone here."

The youngsters do not know each other when they arrive, even though they are all related in the same way. They are bonded by the common thread of cancer, that evil stitch that perhaps has claimed a limb or the wavy hair that once danced along the edge of an open shirt collar. Whatever cancer may have taken from them, Camp Mak-A-Dream offers a chance to forget.

"So where you from?" a visitor asks one of the youngsters who seems slightly removed and to the side of a busy group intent on kicking a soccer ball into remission. "Michigan," the kid replies. "Livonia, Michigan." Another reluctant camper volunteers that he has come from Missoula, fifty miles away.

So why do we come here? One might ask. We come to meet the dream in reality, and dreamers who brought a benign place to life. We come to listen to the sounds of children at play, to hear the words of those children who have grown too old for their years. We come to look into the hearts of two Detroiters who made their personal dream a haven, and a home away from home on this Montana mountainside.

The dream was actually born in western Montana long before it was even conceived. It was born out of a love of the outdoors, the thrill of a seasonal elk hunt, and the solace to be found in watching a sunset paint the majesty of the mountains in its purple hues. On an eighty-seven acre site, carved out of a sprawling ranch owned by a devoted husband and wife from Detroit, Camp Mak-A-Dream would come true.

Good fortune had smiled on Harry and Sylvia Granader. Their life together had been of storybook proportions. He was a successful businessman, outdoorsman, and father. She was an accomplished artisan, a World War II Army Air Force pilot, and a doting mother of five healthy children.

Harry had hooked up with the McDonald's golden arches in franchising's infancy, but the burgers and fries did more than just feed his growing family. As it grew, the restaurant chain had begun opening Ronald McDonald Houses around the country. Attached to medical centers and treatment facilities, the houses provided a place for parents of hospitalized children to stay close to their kids during the long days of therapy and recovery. That's how Harry Granader's personal dream was born.

"We have been so fortunate in our own lives," Harry explains. "We felt we just had to do something for the kids. These are all God's children." His voice chokes with emotion, "You're put here to do something for others…" Harry's voice is suddenly lost in that awkward space between a choke and a tear. Sylvia would rescue the moment, but she can't. "Now Harry, I told you not to get so emotional," she says in the soft tone she probably used on her own children a good many years ago.

It's safe to say Harry doesn't have just a soft spot for kids in his heart; he has a big hole in it for them. It's a hole that hurts, hurts so much he has trouble talking about it and that's when Sylvia usually has just the right words to offer.

The emotion comes often from Harry. It shows all the time, in fact. It's there in the smile; it's in the eyes that wander beyond the window and onto the faces of the children he may know only for a week. But they are the faces of his dream, in a place where they can be kids. A place where they can come together, to share, to laugh, to tease, to cry, to eat, to swim, to run, to ride, to walk, to enjoy that treasured part of childhood upon which cancer has abruptly intruded.

It began in 1993. The rolling acres and the seed money came from Harry and Sylvia. More came from others who supported their dream too, and in 1995, two years after breaking ground on a lonely hillside, Camp Mak-A-Dream raised the flag of welcome to the first of the cancer campers. It was a special moment for two Detroiters a thousand miles from home.

Harry and Sylvia are far more than just benefactors at the camp. In many ways, they are the spirit of the place. Ever present, ever visible, ever there with a word of encouragement, they are perhaps surrogate grandparents, each making sure their special kids get the chance to just be kids. And the children respond in kind with scribbled notes of gratitude and love, carefully tucked into brown paper lunch bags thumb-tacked to a wall that serves as the camp's official post office.

"I love you," the simple note reads in Harry's hand. Doctor Stu, sitting at a table in the empty dining hall muses, "I don't know whether Harry and Sylvia love the kids more, or the kids love Harry and Sylvia more." The smile on his face answers his own rhetorical question.

The years now number well past eighty for the couple who still seems to be honeymooning as they wander around the camp grounds. Harry appears to walk every foot of the trails and paths each day. Of course, that's after he has completed his morning regimen of sit-ups. Sylvia's usually on the move too. Quite often she can be found in her beloved art barn working with a homesick child, perhaps weaving a memory in cloth that both will take home when the winds of autumn once again rush down the rolling hillsides of Gold Creek.

It is appropriately named. Camp Mak-A-Dream is a dream and a place to dream. For Harry and Sylvia Granader, it is their dream come true.

A typical day begins in a typical way on the mountainside. Sleepy-eyed kids are stirred from their bunks, wash up briefly, and then line up for what has become a morning ritual at camp. In a few minutes, they present a modestly rehearsed tribute to the camp cook. You see, it is the cook who will decide just which of the bunkhouse residents will be chosen to be seated and eat first.

There follows a talent show of sorts. Each of the bunkhouses must serve up its sleepers to perform a witty ditty extolling the virtues or even the shortcomings of the food and its preparation that are soon to follow. It is not an easy task to choose among the presenters for they have had little time to write their poems or learn their lyrics to a song or melody that most will quickly forget anyhow.

In studied grace, the camp cook watches the performances and makes a deliberately difficult decision. "Bear Lodge," he announces over the balcony rail. The campers either moan or shout with glee and the rush to breakfast is on.

The victors receive applause and high-fives as they pass through a human tunnel comprised of the camp counselors, volunteers, and staff. The tunnel leads into the dining hall as another day at Camp Mak-A-Dream officially begins.

As a few minutes of after-breakfast calm return to the big lodge, Doctor Stu has some time to call his own. He is one of the many volunteers who find their way to Montana each summer. He happens to come all the way from New York City where he maintains a very busy private practice the rest of the year. But this is vacation time, his time away from the hustle and bustle of the big city. When summer beckons, so does Camp Mak-A-Dream.

"I don't really know why it's become such a thing with me," he tries to explain. "When I was a kid, my parents always sent me off to camp, and I loved the experience and looked forward to it each year. I just love going to camp, and here…it's all so special, I just have to come back. I've come every year. In fact I plan my whole year around coming to Camp Mak-A-Dream. We have a full hospital here on the grounds. We're capable of treating almost any need that arises among the campers. I just have to be here, that's all."

The days are, as one might guess, filled with camp stuff. They're filled with challenges, filled with activities of all sorts, physical, mental, and emotional. They're filled with new friendships, and most of all, filled with encouragement. Each child feeds the other strength to keep going, to keep pushing, to keep trying, because each of them has known the need themselves.

"'Atta boy Will, you can do it…you can make it. Don't look down, just one foot after the other," the words melt in among the other declarations of support for the frightened camper who maneuvers so slowly and carefully along a high wire that stretches between two standing poles erected by some military experts in a clearing beyond the big lodge. The kids are tethered, there is no danger, but the ground might as well be a mile away when you're staring down at it. This is one of the challenges of Camp Mak-A-Dream.

Down the hill and past the stand of matured pine trees, another group gathers in the art center, Sylvia's beloved barn. Some gravitate to the big loom to weave a multicolored swatch of cloth. Others find their way to a nearby table to make a memento of the day. Before they leave camp, they will each make a special ceramic tile that will join many others that line the walls. Each tile contains a brief message or thought from another camper in another year from another week at Camp Mak-A-Dream. It is a tactile expression in acrylic paint and heartfelt thought that says "I was here too. I shared the dream."

While the eighty-seven acres that comprise the camp may seem remote by urban standards, the camp is close to a number of nearby towns. The camp is also close to the hearts of the people who live in those small towns. On this particular day in July, the unmistakable rumble of Chevrolet Corvettes is carried on the wind as some of the locals arrive to take the kids on a two-seat, fuel-injected joyride around the Montana countryside.

A few hours later, some much more sedate transportation lumbers up the hillside to take the campers over to another town that cares about them. It's maybe thirty or forty miles, as the eagle flies, over to little Phillipsburg. A group of parents in the town have cooked up a barbecue in the park especially for their annual summer guests. It's hot—nearly ninety degrees—and shade is at a premium, but the kids are front and center in this well-planned show of western hospitality.

After the burgers and the sloppy joes are gone, after the watermelon seeds have all been spit out, after the ice cream has melted on the cone and found its way down to a spot in the middle of the tee-shirt, the campers are treated to a stage show in the old opera house. A full day in the mountain air soon calls the campers back to the lodge that has become a new home in just a couple of days.

Without even looking, one can find magic in this place. Perhaps it is the majesty of unspoiled nature. Perhaps the magic is distilled in the profound peace one senses in the almost infinite silence of the mountains. Whatever it is, it seems to invade the soul and refresh it. That would seem to be reason enough to build a camp of dreams here, and certainly it is reason enough for the children of cancer to come and seek it.

"Magic comes from within," one child wrote on the face of her ceramic tile, "and if your heart can know this magic, share it with all kids." The mature words of a fifth-grader named Michelle.

It is magic that both permeates and perpetuates the camp. It is the magic of charity, the magic of a hundred volunteers, and the magic of dedication to an idea. It is simply the magic of sharing life with a few of the very young who might not get the chance to enjoy life's full measure and potential. Camp Mak-A-Dream dwells neither in the past nor in the future. It lives for today.

So what does a week cost in the hills above Gold Creek? Nothing! It is free to those who can come and that is the magic of charity. That is the reward for those whose contributions and donations make it possible each year. For the counselors, the group leaders, and the volunteers, warm hearts create the magical chance to know an effervescent kid from Michigan named Mikey, or a quiet serious child named Will from Detroit, or a young woman named Kathy from South Lyon, or four dozen others just like them.

Those who study such things tell us our children are growing up too fast these days. They tell us the basic elements, the very essences of childhood, are being jettisoned as we rocket our way along the uncharted pathways of the information age. That's not happening in Gold Creek. Being a child will always be job one at Camp Mak-A-Dream, even if the child has packed too much maturity into his or her backpack.

Sadly, summer ends too quickly each year in the peaks of the Montana mountains. For the campers, a week seems to evaporate more quickly than the perspiration acquired in the heat of a good old-fashioned sack race. But, as somebody once said, all good things must come to an end. So with a few songs and some lengthy tales of the old west, Cowboy Bob, a local entertainer, brings down the curtain on another full week at Camp Mak-A-Dream.

As the sun settles quietly beyond the rim of the distant hilltops, the campers, the counselors, and the friends of the camp all gather to sit in the glow of a traditional campfire. Encircled by several teepees that reflect the amber tones of the fading light, the group sings the camp song. They sit, side by side, shoulder to shoulder, some on a counselor's lap, to celebrate the days that have come before this one. It is a time of reflection for each.

It has been a chance to be a real kid again. A chance to sleep out under a cream cheese Montana moon. A chance to drop into a patch of grass and try to catch a falling star. It has been a chance to wonder at the wonder of life.

For Harry and Sylvia Granader, who dared to make a dream come true, another rewarding day ends in the fading embers of the fire. For Mikey and Will, for Kathy and Michelle, for Doctor Stu, it has been a day of sharing in the dream that lives each day along the Clark Fork River in Gold Creek, Montana.

Marriage

A Visit to Santa

It doesn't look much like the North Pole. You won't find any reindeer running around in the backyard. There aren't any elves to be found in the shop either, at least I didn't see any of them when I dropped by. All I found were two of Santa's full-time helpers hard at work on a humid summer morning, getting ready for another Christmas season.

Christmas comes about three hundred days a year here. Where is here, you ask? Well, it's just about eighty miles north of Detroit—as the reindeer flies—then you turn left into some heavy woods, wander along a path that seems to lead to nowhere, and you'll find it. Then you've got to find Santa's helpers.

They're usually out there in back, in the shop carving or maybe painting away on one of the many likenesses of their boss. Vaughn and Stephanie Rawson probably know as much about old Santa Claus as anybody on this good earth. Why? Because they live with him almost every day!

"You know, Santa produces such a good feeling to all people," Vaughn quickly exclaims. "For most of us, it's a favorite time of the year, and for Stephanie and me, it lasts all year."

Vaughn Rawson officially calls himself the "Whimsical Whittler." At least that's the official name of his present occupation. He has always had an affinity for wood, combined with a passion for American history. It's not surprising then that he has made just about every stick of furniture in this special house at the North Pole of Michigan. He likes making stuff, antique stuff that isn't really antique but looks that way.

It was a few years back when Vaughn was doing a little bit of whittling on a piece of wood, that he suddenly thought he began to see the face of Santa Claus in there. So he carved around the grain, smoothed an edge or two, and sure enough there it was, his first version of Kris Kringle.

The truth is, he didn't think very much of that first effort, so he decided to make another one. Then he made another one, and another one, and then another one. After a dozen or so, old Santa had changed his life.

"It's a challenge," Vaughn says with a smile, not unlike the smile you see on one of his carvings. "You have to see him in there, in that flat block of wood and then bring him out."

I guess you might say Santa Claus has made a lot of decisions for the Christmas couple. Vaughn and Stephanie once had good jobs with the State of Michigan; they had the pension plan, the health insurance, and the job security that goes with government employment. But it was Santa who whispered in their ears one day, and soon they decided to quit the real world and jump on the back of the magic sleigh that would carry them off and into a brand-new world of real-life fantasy.

"It was an opportunity to do something totally differ- ent," Vaughn explains. "When all is said and done, it was probably the best thing that could ever happen to me; it was the chance to become a full-time wood carver."

Vaughn's carefully carved Santa figures had struck a Christmas chord in those who saw them in the early days. He sold them as quickly as he could create them, each delicately carved from a piece of basswood. It is tedious work employing the tools of the special trade which haven't changed significantly since the legend of Saint Nicholas was born.

Each year, Vaughn Rawson carves a different face and form. Each of the figures is artfully tinted and stained with Stephanie's gentle touch. The pieces bear the aged look of the old world, the look of Christmases long since past as they are readied for their individual journeys around the world to new homes. Most will arrive as a holiday present intended to last for many holidays into the future.

"I almost feel like they are my children," the whimsical whittler admits. "But I know they're going to good homes where they will be part of Christmas celebrations for years and years to come."

If their happy hands stay busy, the Rawson team may complete as many as five hundred Santas from one Christ- mas until the next. The wooden figurines are considered collector's items now. Most of them are pre-ordered and sold before their design has even been imagined. The Santas have become so famous that the White House has been hanging them on the national Christmas tree in Washington.

"We even have a picture of Bill and Hillary Clinton posing in front of the tree. See, right above Bill's right ear. It almost looks like he's whispering something to him," Vaughn says with an obvious chuckle.

When the holidays are over, Santa's Michigan helpers usually try to take a little break from their hectic North Pole chores. Santa does allow them to work on their own schedule, after all. They may do a little traveling in January each year, but it's not very long before the voice of Mr. Claus is calling them back into the woodshop to begin the task of getting the spirit of Christmas back in shape for another season that will come all too quickly.

It seems safe to say that if anyone truly knows how to keep the spirit of Christmas in their hearts all year long, it must be Vaughn and Stephanie Rawson.

"You know, the holidays come and go around here," Vaughn says. "New Year's, Easter, Memorial Day, Fourth of July, Labor Day; they all come and go...but it's always Christmas Day at our house."

A Stitch in Time

Marc Miller is seated in a comfortable round-backed chair in the small parlor of his Marine City home. He is doing what he loves best: stitching on an antique reproduction sampler. Rarely a day goes by when his hands are not pushing or pulling a colored thread through a piece of linen that will one day tell a story from the past to the future.

It is tedious and time-consuming work, but Marc has the time now. Far more time, in fact, than he was given back in 1996 when his doctors told him he had terminal brain cancer.

"By all accounts, I shouldn't be here…but I am." He says with speech that has been altered, but not stolen entirely by his ordeal with the unthinkable.

In September of 1996, Marc's passion for his needle and thread suddenly waned. He had just begun his twenty-fifth year of teaching school, but this new school year would last only five days. He was barely forty-six years old when the doctors told him he was the victim of lymphoma of the central nervous system, a very rare and very aggressive form of brain cancer. They sadly told him there were few, if any, treatment options. Yes, some chemo might buy a little extra time, or it could take some away. The family went home to talk.

It is hard to imagine the conversation that followed, but Marc and Jo Miller made the choice. Marc would come home to die. Jo even assumed the dreadful task of making funeral arrangements for her living husband. Hospice was invited and with an abiding faith in their God, the days slipped into weeks, and the days into months, until they reached Marc's forty-seventh birthday.

He was back in Ann Arbor for another evaluation. The doctors talked, examined, tested, and were confounded. The cancer was gone. "They said they couldn't find it anywhere…" his voice trails off in the wonder of it all. Jo's eyes swell as she listens to the halting words that tell of a miracle.

There is simply no medical explanation, no scientific analysis, no recent precedent in oncology, perhaps no words in the English language that can be summoned to account for Marc Miller's apparent recovery. There is only one word, and Marc knows it. "It's God's miracle," he says without hesitation.

The miracle of Marc had been eighteen months in the making. In September of 1997, he once again picked up a piece of linen, his needle, and colored threads, and began to stitch again. Only now, he stitched free of fear, free of pain, free of the cancer that had ravaged his mind and body, and in its deadly process had nearly snatched his life.

"I am a walking miracle," he says from the rollback chair. "I can't say it any differently. I thank God every day, when I say my prayers, I say 'Thank you for letting me be here today.'" His words tumble from his mouth in the excitement. "You know, I haven't had a headache since 1996."

Wife Jo, seated a few feet away, keeps herself from assuming the role of interpreter when Marc's speech falters or his context becomes fuzzy. She knows her husband is back, but he's not all the way back. "We take each day as a gift," she says with conviction. "This was all meant to be. That is our perspective." Marc pushes another green thread into the beige piece of linen, seeming oblivious to the words being spoken a few feet from his feet.

Marc's delicate samplers hang in every room of the Millers' house. He has done scores of them over the years. His skilled work has been displayed in a number of Americana shows, and one hangs in the Port Huron, Michigan museum. Sadly, however, his most treasured piece vanished while he was on a visit to the University of Michigan Hospital in Ann Arbor. It was the story of Marc's childhood, told in needlepoint. He created it to be an heirloom for his two young sons. It was Daddy's life story in a million hand-sewn stitches, and suddenly it was gone.

"We were sitting in a waiting room at the hospital, and Marc was using the time to do a little work on the sampler. I guess he must have put it down when we were called. When we came back, it was gone." Jo doesn't and won't assign blame for the heirloom's disappearance. "I don't think anybody would take it deliberately—maybe they didn't know what it was; maybe they didn't know how much meaning it had."

Calls to the hospital, even other visits to the waiting room have yielded nothing in their search for the missing cloth. "It wasn't quite finished," Jo continues to explain.

"It had Marc's dogs, the pond where he used to swim as a boy..." There were lots of green threads in the grass of the memories stitched one by one.

For Marc and Jo, it's not about the three hundred hours of sewing, it's not about the single hour that was left to finish the canvas in cloth, it's about them, their hearts, Marc's life, the memories in thread, just suddenly gone without a trace. "It's a lot of sentiment, I know, but it was Marc's gift to our children. It's just sad for all of us."

To this day, no trace of Marc's treasured sampler has ever turned up. To Marc and Jo it was irreplaceable, and he says he won't or can't make another one.

Despite their melancholy over the loss of the unique sampler, life goes on at the Miller house in Marine City. Things are different, of course, because no journey in life comes without some cost. From the depths of an impenetrable coma to the unbridled joy of restored consciousness, from the clutches of a wheelchair to the relative freedom of a cane, from the doorway of death to the promise of extended life, they have walked together with their God. It has been an exhausting, exhilarating, and enriching experience.

Do they believe in miracles? You bet they do, and they hope you do too, because they're living one.

"It's so easy for all of us to forget what we have," Jo Miller concludes. "These days are all numbered. Enjoy each one of them."

No Strangers to the Woods

It is dawn, and the family is gathering together once again. As the first beams of sunlight spill across the marsh, deep in the quiet of the silent woods, they exchange glances. Their long friendship has brought an uncommon trust to this place. It is an awkward trust that culminates in a truly unique union between two separate worlds—the infinite and mysterious space where man and animal are related. For some fleeting moments, they are a family, sharing time and circumstance, proximity and affection, separated simply by creation's grand design.

"Come here, little one…yes, you're looking bright eyed this morning." The words drop to the ground in the muffling silence that surrounds them. Carl speaks as if talking to a child who has suddenly entered a room full of familiar strangers. His camera rests in the dew drops that are sprinkled about in the morning grass.

It is another day when the white tails, the chickadees, the awkward fawns, the blue jay, the cardinal, the mourning dove, and the princely buck find themselves in an unlikely union with Carl Sams and Jean Stoic. It is a reunion ritual, timed to a shutter's snap.

59

For years they have come to this special place, tucked away off a busy road that meanders through the vastness of nature that is Kensington Metropark. They have come to see the wild and the wild things in it. They have come bearing gifts of carrots, nuts, and seeds. They also carry with them two cameras and a heartfelt appreciation and love for the nature that surrounds them in this favorite place.

"We try to come here at least two or three times a week," says Carl as he peers through the single-lens reflex viewfinder. "It doesn't matter what time of the year, we try to get out here to visit...to say hello, to stay acquainted and familiar."

Carl and Jean, as you might have guessed, are wildlife photographers. They have traveled the world in search of the perfect picture in nature. There are sixty or maybe seventy thousand of them in their staggering portfolio. But it is in Kensington Park, almost in their own backyard, that acclaim and honor have suddenly found them. One might say the have been discovered in the pages of a children's picture book, a photographic fantasy that they have titled *Stranger in the Woods*.

"It started with a friend's suggestion," Carl says as he recalls the book's beginnings. "We had all of these photographs of a snowman that we built in the woods."
Jean chimes in on the story. "It was just an idea, to see how the birds and the deer might react to the snowman that was suddenly in their midst."

It was a snowman with a traditional carrot nose, walnut eyes, and a capful of cracked corn and sunflower seed. Who would have guessed that it was the very beginning of a publishing success story? The curious denizens of the marsh, the meadow, and the hollows in the oak trees came to visit the iceman who had so suddenly ventured into their special realm. They came with some obvious misgivings. They came with curious eyes and inquiring noses. They snatched a corn kernel from the stocking cap, only to alight on a branch to dine and peer once again at the stranger who was so boldly standing in their woods. As they came, the cameras claimed each moment.

"It was such fun to watch," Jean explains, the excitement still fresh in her speech. "We had the pictures, so then we needed a story to tie it all together." The words soon followed and the photo fantasy was on its way to reality in the competitive world of children's publishing.

The little snowman and his friends in the woods soon captured the eyes and the imaginations of children and their parents around the globe. In a matter of months, the self-published book had climbed the bestseller lists for children, and Carl and Jean were suddenly thrust headlong into the publishing business. Lavish praise was coming from many quarters, including some very prestigious awards, all of which combined to turn their modest home in Milford, Michigan into a basement computer empire.

Unfortunately, success never comes without a hefty price tag. The little snowman has taken them, at least for a time, out of some of their favorite wild places and into the less natural environs of the celebrity world: a place where they are not as comfortable.

The success of the book does have its rewards, of course. They have turned over generous portions of the book sales to a number of children's causes and environmental protection efforts.

While the stranger in the woods has made them familiar faces in the book business, Carl and Jean are trying hard not to become strangers in their own woods these days. They're trying not to be too far away from their extended family of furry and feathered friends in the Kensington meadows. They still insist on making regular visits to the spot where the snowman was born, despite the grueling public demands that sudden success too often brings to the unsuspecting.

In what has become a very personal crusade, the two photographer-authors have waged a battle recently to protect their beloved deer family from the annual culling of the over-populated herd that actually threatens their wild place. At least for now their family of whitetails, young and old, remains intact.

Soon the cycles of the seasons will again be focused in the lenses of their cameras. The rolls of film will be filled with the images of a thousand of nature's special moments, stolen away just for us who cannot live in their unique world, but who can share in it through their eyes, and who can help them protect it for the future.

Carl Sams and Jean Stoic truly believe there is a snowman to be found in each of us.

Cruisin' Woodward

There are a million stories in the Woodward Dream Cruise and this is just one of them. It's a love story that began with an awkward dance in the eighth grade, endured half a lifetime of separation, and finally culminated in a storybook reunion over forty years later.

This is the story of a little girl named Patty O'Connor and a red-haired boy named Denny Flynn who grew up together in a Royal Oak neighborhood, and fell in love when they danced the night away in junior high.

Remembering the night, Denny said: "I was too shy to ask her, and by the time I did ask her, she already had a date. So I went to the dance without a date and danced every dance with her. Of course her date got mad and left, so I got to take her home."

Patty and Denny dated all through high school, but in 1961, Denny joined the Navy. They thought about getting married, decided to wait, and then time and distance took their toll on two young lives. "I got out in October 1962, the day of the Cuban missile crisis. I stayed in California for about six months and then I came home and asked about

Patty. They said 'Oh, she's engaged' and I thought 'darn it' and we both got on with our lives."

Patty eventually married someone else, and so did Denny, who packed up and moved west to Colorado. Time passed and two separate lives were lived out without contact. Ultimately, however, both of their marriages floundered.

While he was living out west, Denny happened to find his dream car in Colorado Springs. It was a 1971 Chevy SS that needed, well, a little work. So he carefully restored it and then in the summer of 1996, he drove it back to Royal Oak for a visit with his parents. That was, of course, the year of the second—what would become annual—Woodward Dream Cruise. Little did Denny know that along Woodward Avenue that day, fate was about to get his motor really running.

As Denny recalls it:

> A guy saw the Colorado tags on my plates and says, "You came all the way from Colorado for this cruise?"
>
> I said, "Well I grew up here and I went to school here and everything." I don't know what made me say it, but I added, "While I'm here, I always check up on an old girlfriend."
>
> So he says "What's your name?"
>
> "Denny Flynn."
>
> "I'm Harry Sprat, we went to school together."
>
> Then his wife perks up and she says, "I'm Mary Beth O'Connell, and I was one or your sister's best friends. Who's this gal you're talking about?"

I said, "Well, I don't know her married name, but her maiden name was Patty O'Connor."

Mary Beth replied, "She got a divorce about two years ago and she lives out in Whitmore Lake."

Well, it didn't take long; Denny and Patty had a date for dinner. After more than three decades had passed, the childhood sweethearts would meet again in the glow of a warm August sunset at the lake.

Denny knows it by heart. "When we were eating dinner I said, 'Patty, I've gotta show you something' and I pulled out my wallet. I had laminated her high school picture after graduation, and I carried it in my wallet all of those years."

Did they talk about marriage at that point? "Oh, yeah," says Patty.

Denny quickly interrupts, "I just think I knew that night at the lake. The sun was going down behind her and I had the harpoon right through me. I reminded her that I had asked her in 1961 to marry me and I said, 'Have you made up your mind yet?'"

Well, you can guess the rest of this story. After the wedding vows were exchanged after all those years, you know they had to drive off into the sunset in the red Chevy. Yes, the '71 SS will be in the Woodward Dream Cruise this year, and next year, and the year after, the year after—because this is, after all, a fairy tale.

It's the tale of the Snow White of Saint Mary's School and her Prince Charming who arrived at her doorstep in a shiny red Chevrolet. Now, don't you just have to believe they will live happily ever after? I do.

Laurie's Letter

It was a couple days after Christmas when Laurie McCormick sat down and began to write her letter to me. I read it a few days later on New Year's Eve.

"Dear Erik," she wrote, "I would like to make you aware of two very special people. They are both physically challenged due to birth defects. One has cerebral palsy and the other spina bifida. As a result, one has been confined to a wheelchair for more than forty years. The life they have led is extraordinary to say the very least and should truly be an inspiration to others. Oh, by the way Erik, they happen to be my parents, Dick and Jean Beer of Lake Orion, Michigan."

Laurie's letter continued. "My parents have been married for forty-three years, each dealing with the trials and tribulations that life has dealt them. My father worked as the Oakland County Law Librarian for thirty-five years, and my mother raised one very active and very normal daughter. They have lived and cared for a house that was custom built for my mother's wheelchair about thirty-seven years ago."

The images in the letter were starting to become clear: This was an exceptional couple. Laurie's letter wasn't finished. "I'm not just writing because they are my parents. They are an inspiration to all who cross their paths because of their zest for living a full life even when faced with the daily challenges their limitations present. They put all of us without such challenges to shame." It was time to pay a visit to Lake Orion.

A long way north on M-24, past the Pistons' Palace, the county parks, and a dozen car dealerships, Jean and Richard Beer live in a modest ranch home, settled on a street that runs atop the rolling terrain of the Oakland County countryside.

When we arrive, they are busy doing normal, everyday tasks. Jean is in the kitchen, finishing up some dishes from breakfast. Dick is in the den, deliberately working some keystrokes on the computer. To the visitor's eye, there are some geometric calculations that don't work in the house. It is spatially disconcerting, almost Lilliputian in concept. For instance, the kitchen counter is less than a yardstick high.

"Isn't this unusual?" chirps Jean from the comfort of her wheelchair. Behind her big glasses, the eyes sparkle and seem to radiate fun. Her husband of so many years sits nearby, sipping on a mug of coffee. His hands shake in the edgy rhythm of the palsied. He too welcomes the visitors gracefully, but in words that come with much greater effort.

"There is so much more I could say," continues Laurie in her letter. "One thing that really sparked my interest in writing to you: Over the holidays, my parents like to go shopping, each in their own powered wheelchairs, cruising the mall together, and at times, separately. One of their gifts to each other last year was a set of two-way radios so they can talk to each other when they are out together."

She describes an incident in the mall, when Dick and Jean have become separated. After all, one does not want the other to see what they're buying for presents.

"Where are you?" Dick asks into the handheld radio.

"I'm over by the Penney's store," comes the answer Dick needed.

"Okay, I'll meet you there in a minute. Wait for me there." There's nothing covert about the conversation, but they do look like a couple of secret agents or undercover mall security. Within minutes, the Beers are reunited and off in their matching power chairs to another section of the shopping center.

At home, the shopping for the day done, there is time for some quiet time. Now, there are few moments to deflect and defy the stereotypes of the physically challenged. "We just do what everybody else does," says Jean, her eyes sparkling once again with the sheer joy of her explanation. We live, we work, and we celebrate the holidays just like everybody else."

Richard looks on and nods in agreement as Jean continues to expand on her thought. "It's worked so well for us because I can't walk." She points at her husband, "He can." Richard nods in affirmation as Jean continues. "Now, his arms don't work so well, and mine do. So you see, we're really just one entity."

A large piano, perhaps a grand or baby grand, dominates the living room. On its surface rests a gathering of family photographs: pictures of Dick and Jean in younger days, and several pictures of Laurie, whose letter has led us to this opportunity to share two improbable but wonderfully possible lives. Laurie has spent many hours at the keyboard.

"I'm so very proud to have such wonderful people in my life," she says, not as a daughter, but as a cheerleader for the challenged. "When I have a bad day, I just look at them and realize…" She doesn't need any more words to complete the sentence. "I've just always wanted someone to tell their story…"

Laurie finishes her letter. "There is just so much more I could say because there are so many more stories about my parents. I hope I haven't wasted your time. Happy Holidays, Sincerely, Laurie McCormick."

You know, I never really answered her letter…but when I do, maybe it should go something like this. "No Laurie, you didn't waste a moment of our time, and thanks so very much for writing."

Passions

Buzzin' Bears

What's that sound you're hearing? Oh, it's her again. No, she's not a chip off the old block. She is a homemaker, a wife, and a hard-working mother with an uncontrollable passion for chainsaws and bears. Big bears, little bears, it doesn't matter. She sees bears everywhere. They are the bears she sees in the woods. They are the bears she can find in dead trees, or peeling stumps, or broken limbs scattered along a rural roadway. They are the bears that live anywhere she can find a good piece of wood.

Angela Orr is a chainsaw artist. She is one of the few female members of a small club generally dominated by members of the other gender. So, what's a nice young woman like this doing with a mean, noisy, rip-slashing, nasty, tree-eating, bush-whacking saw with more teeth than a grizzly bear? Well, she's looking for bears again.

"I tell ya, there's a bear just screaming to get out of every log," the gentle Angela says as she yanks the pull cord on the stubborn orange saw. This time she has to yank it twice.

Angie has quite an assortment of chainsaws. Michelangelo, after all, had his complement of brushes and paint and hammers and chisels. So it shouldn't be a surprise that an artist of this century would need a collection of cutting tools particularly suited to the varieties of wood she will encounter in her quest to find the perfect bear.

"There's no such thing as a mistake when you're carving wood with a chainsaw," Angela patiently explains. "You just keep cutting until you're done, until you're satisfied with the way it all looks."

Behind the protective goggles, Angie's eyes search for the elusive features that seem, to my eyes, to be extremely well hidden in the swirling grain behind and around all of those pesky knotholes. Come out, come out, wherever you are so we can see you. Can you see the bear?

When she's not busy at home taking care of the kids, or making dinner, or maybe painting the barn, Angela is often out on the road displaying her work at an art show, where she will sell her stuff or take on a commission or two from somebody who happens to have a dead tree in their yard. Sitting still is not one of Angela's favorite pastimes.

"I don't know, it's just something inside of me," she says with all the honesty of a country girl next door. "Those chainsaws are my jewelry, I guess. Diamonds are supposed to be a girl's best friend, but I think chainsaws are mine."

It's no surprise that Angie's husband Steve is her number-one fan and a dependable personal assistant. He knows how to sharpen a chain, replace a stubborn pull cord or fix a fouled spark plug. Not that Angie doesn't know how to do those jobs, it's just a family affair at the Orr place.

"It really does come from my heart," she says, her blue eyes twinkling. "I guess you could make a big deal out of it, but for me, it's just a lot of fun."

Angie's roaring saws don't always find bears in the woods. Quite often she'll find some other critter lurking inside one of the rings of age that tell her some of the secrets of the tree stump's past. It's just that bears are her favorites. Maybe they're easier to spot.

"It's just like a musician," Angie says. "You practice and you practice, and the more you practice the better you get. I get out here and I start carving and the world kind of goes away. I guess it's like therapy for me."

No matter, the bear with the friendly eyes and the warm mouth is something of an Angie Orr trademark. So, the next time you're driving along a Michigan country road and you happen to spot a bear clinging to the side of an old dead tree, or maybe peeking around at you from a long-neglected stump, you'll know in your heart that Angela Orr from Fowlerville was probably in the neighborhood.

Blues from the Lowlands

He sits behind a large console with a turntable and tone-arm at arm's length. The music flows under as he begins another Saturday morning with the blues. "Good morning...welcome to Blues from the Lowlands," the baritone voice intones.

His name is Robert B. Jones, the teacher, preacher, historian, singer, and storyteller. Those are some of his many calling cards, but we'll just call him Robert Jones, the bluesman, who is Detroit's personal custodian of an African-American treasure in music.

"It's time to leave the mountains of the Carolinas and head on to the Mississippi delta and the music of Big Joe Williams, played on that unique-sounding twelve-string guitar."

For years, if you happened to listen to WDET-FM, Detroit's public radio, every Saturday morning you would hear Robert, perhaps explaining the history of an obscure recording of a song born somewhere in the backwash of the delta or the foothills of the rural south. This is the time for Robert Jones, the musical historian.

"The late Son House whose work was so influential to so many. A man who lived out his final years in virtual seclusion right here in our own Motor City."

Should you happen into a public school and hear an acoustic guitar and the voices of some children echoing down an empty hallway, you will not only hear, but you will see Robert Jones the teacher and the historian keeping the music of generations past alive for the generations of today.

"If I take that old blues song, put my guitar down, and just speed up the words with a different beat, what have I got?"

Robert quickly repeats the words of the song, adding a little facial expression, a little body language with the hands stabbing the air in front of his chest. The question clearly posed, the wide-eyed youngsters respond in ear-piercing unison, "It's rap!" The discovery brings forth a cascade of smiles and instant recognition to the young faces who have suddenly found something of their own in something that just moments ago seemed so very old.

Perhaps if you attend a local arts festival, or you frequent one of the local concert venues, you will personally get the opportunity to experience one of those moments with Robert Jones, the singer, the instrumentalist, the Baptist minister who preaches the gospel, and carries in his guitar case—the bible of the blues.

"The blues is African American in the truest sense of both words," the teacher tells us. "It is a snapshot of life past and present."

For Robert Jones, the road to those many classrooms, to the stages, to the microphones, and to the pulpit of the church, began with an old pawnshop guitar and the love of the music his ancestors left behind to ring in his heart. He had no idea back then where the six strings on that old guitar were going to take him.

"It's a 1933 National steel guitar. When I look at it, I realize how it has enabled me to go places, to see people, to experience the way others live, to understand how music really is the one force that can bring us all together."

The music, the lyrics, and yes, the blues, have taken Robert on a good many journeys around the nation. These days, he's always busy. There are the college seminars to conduct, his Blues for the Schools program continues to fascinate thousands of children, and there is the radio show on Saturday mornings, and don't forget the many concert dates he squeezes in each year. It's a full schedule for the incomparable musician who lives in a time warp of past, present, and future.

He's simply complicated, this man we have come to know as Detroit's Goodwill Ambassador of the Blues.

"I'm not sure why I'm the mix I am," he says reflectively. "It must just be what God intended."

Detroit's Grill King

Since 1983, a little-used alleyway just south of Eight Mile Road has served as the world headquarters of the Robert Felton Institute of Grillology.

"Man, just like Versace was to clothes, that's what I am to the grill," Mr. Felton proudly exclaims.

From his humble shop, in which he can't park his car anymore, has come a steady stream of 55-gallon drum-size barbecue grills. Each is decked out in a layer of flat black high-temperature paint and enough spot welds to make a Ford Model T envious.

As you can well imagine, when summer can be found on the calendar page, Robert's in overdrive. Well, the truth is, Robert's always in overdrive. That's just the entrepreneurial spirit coming through at full throttle.

The Felton Institute, of which he is CEO, President, and managing partner, turns out barbecue grills from refurbished 16-gauge oil barrels. He swears the best thing to cook on one of his babies is a big ol' T-bone steak.

To his neighbors, friends, and pure barbecue aficionados

everywhere, Robert is known as Detroit's Grill King. He even has red and white lawn signs printed up that stake his claim to the title. Like those obnoxious political signs at election time, they're everywhere. But they work.

As you might guess, the Felton Grillology enterprise is basically a mom-and-pop operation. Robert designs and welds. His patient wife polishes and paints. The kids stay the heck out of the way because Robert's always on the move.

In his two decades in the backyard barbecue business, the Grill King has had his shares of ups and downs, but he's convinced again this year that things are heating up. He has plans to move the operation out of his old garage and into an old factory warehouse. It's a big step up, trust me.

In many ways, Robert thinks of himself as sort of the Henry Ford of the barrel barbecue business. After all, he laughs, "Mr. Ford started out in a funky, beat up ol' garage too and look what he done for this country." That's the spirit I'm talking about.

It has always been his dream to own his own business, Robert will eagerly tell you. "I have a dream" he says. "One of my dreams is a real manufacturing facility. I want to see jobs, man." With the hope of the new factory warehouse fresh in his mind, he wants to streamline his assembly process and add some employees. Okay, it's a big dream from the big guy who has never been afraid of work.

Robert hopes that if things work out, he can produce more than his current operating level of about one thousand grills a year. He has already sold them from Bloomfield to Belleville, but he thinks he's still a long way from rolling his barrels into the really big backyard barbecue market in and around Detroit. One of these days, he wants to put them in a

Kmart or maybe a Home Depot where he's convinced they'll revolutionize the summer picnic or family reunion.

Right now he's working on some variations on the oil drum theme. He's got a super grill you could cook a horse in, an all-new propane-friendly version for those too lazy to fire up the charcoal briquettes, as well as his own line of complementary cooking utensils.

I forgot to mention that Robert is also going to market his own special barbecue sauce. He hasn't come up with a name for it yet, but that should be easy. Fact is, he smothered my T-bone in it, and it was, as Lawrence Welk might say, "wunnerful, wunnerful."

By the way, until the Felton Institute does officially relocate, you can get in touch with him on his website or just give him a call at (313) 368-2766 and hold on, because there'll be a tornado on the other end of the line!

Hats by Mertize

The past forty years have not been very kind to the stretch of Woodward Avenue that runs from Warren south to Grand Circus Park. More doors have closed along the street than have opened, more people have left than have come, but on the corner of Peterboro Street still survives what may well be Detroit's last true millinery shop.

It is a genteel and quiet little place where a woman's hat perches easily on a pedestal tree, just waiting for the day when its new owner will appear at the front door. This is the shop that Mertize built with thimbles and thread, straw and silk flowers, and a heart full of determination.

She is the never-mad-hatter, who for over fifty years now has been making heads turn with her unique creations.

"Now, I want you to look in the mirror there." It's not a command, just a gentle suggestion from the woman whose shop bears her name. The customer responds, turning head from side to side, her eyes searching in the mirror for the answer to the same question we all ask ourselves when confronting our image in the truthfulness of glass. Her eyes pleased with the response, she hands the hat to Mertize to be boxed and purchased.

In her decades of hand sewing, Mertize has managed to outlast the fickleness of the fashion world. From her small shop, she has forged a faithful customer base around the country, deeply rooted in the traditions of the Baptist church. On a Sunday morning, one can rest assured that someone, somewhere in America, will be wearing a Mertize original.

"This is what I've been doing all my life," says the hat-maker as she stops for a few moments to ponder what her fingers have brought to life. "It's just what I always wanted to do...way back when I was a little girl, I've been making hats." She chuckles at the thought, perhaps a bit ill at ease about the attention being brought to her chosen work.

When she's not busy making a new hat, Mertize is usually teaching someone else to make a new hat. Daughter Audrey Hawkins wasn't about to get caught up in her mother's specialized business, but it happened anyway. Now Audrey is hoping to take her own creations beyond the strict confines of the church and into the far more secular realms of show business.

"Oh, I'd love to see Aretha Franklin in one of my hats," chirps Audrey, who is obviously far more interested in hats than she ever thought she was going to be. "My style is...well, more youthful, more high spirited, you know, more suited to the entertainment business," she says as if we need an explanation for that unusual space which always rests between generations.

There will never be an assembly line at Mertize Millinery. It just wouldn't work. When each creation is an original, there are no patterns to follow. There are only colors to co-ordinate, textures to counterpoint, a hundred random ideas to be gathered in the tip of a sharp needle, weaving through a straw flower, a feather, or a piece of lace, an idea that will find its way back and forth a thousand times to the dimple of a silver thimble. It is work not suited to a time clock, but work enjoyed by Mertize each and every minute.

"I guess we don't really have a busy season, as such," Mertize explains. "I would say from Easter Sunday on, we're busy, busy, busy." It would be sheer folly to try to describe a hat by Mertize. They are not the dainty pillboxes that Jackie Kennedy made famous. They are not the extra wide chapeaux of 1930s Hollywood; they are simply unique ideas from Mertize that suit the mature ladies of the church to perfection. "I don't even keep a pattern for one I like," she says once again with that chuckle in her voice. "No two alike…that's all." Her gaze returns to the needle in her hand which is attaching a glittered spiral to a satin wrap which surrounds the lower rim of the hat crown.

Yet another generation has joined the happy hat makers at Woodward and Peterboro. Mertize's granddaughter, now old enough to push a needle through some straw by herself, has found the magic and satisfaction that accompanies something beautiful made with her own hand. Is the master preparing for the day when she can put her needle and thread away?

"Oh, no, I'll sew forever," Mertize says, this time with a belly laugh as opposed to her nervous chuckle. "No, no…I'm gonna live to be a hundred and I'll still be making hats." Her attention quickly shifts to a customer who stands in front of a full-length mirror, asking the question in the glass. The answer comes from Mertize. "Oh, you know that pink is a really good color for you." Another Mertize original has just found a new owner.

And so it goes along a weathered stretch of storefronts and plywood windows, Mertize Millinery continues to defy not just changing fad and fashion, but time itself.

Gentle Ben

He is a legend in a very special game. He is a legend without fanfare, without accolade, and without much recognition beyond the few who know his real history.

Well over six decades ago, a young Detroiter named Ben Davis spotted something that was ultimately to take him on his life's journey. It was a tranquil piece of real estate, nestled near a developing area just north of the city. It was a place called Rackham. A municipal golf course lined with stately elm trees, which in the years to come would fall victim to disease and disappear.

Ben Davis fell in love that day and stayed the rest of his life. He hit a few balls in the ensuing weeks and soon caught the eye of the course pro who told him, "As well as you hit the ball, you could teach people how to play." You see, Ben was a natural.

In those days, the closed world of golf had not yet opened its doors to non-Caucasians. With the encouragement of the club pro, Ben was sneaking in the back door. "I said, okay, I'll teach," says the young man with the sweet swing. "And that's how it started. For fifty cents a lesson, I taught. But I could only teach black people."

In the era of Tiger Woods, it's probably difficult for the young to understand what it was like for a proud man like Ben Davis: what it was like to have a natural talent denied, an opportunity missed simply because of color and the prevailing prejudice of the times.

Ben couldn't play on most of the courses around metropolitan Detroit. Oh, he could teach others of color to play the game, but they couldn't play a round of golf anywhere either. Still, Ben says he didn't resent that.

"I just said, to each his own. I've never been the type that pushed for anything. I don't push for nuthin'. If you don't want me, I don't want you. That's just the way I am. I've always been that way." Just the same, one can sense what might have been in his carefully chosen works.

Officially, Ben Davis retired from teaching golf way back in 1972. So why is a man well in his eighth decade of life still taking on students? Well, it doesn't hurt to make a few bucks he says, and there's the fact that he's still in love with the game and the special art of helping people play it well.

Don't get me wrong here. When I say Ben Davis is a legend without the trappings, his passion and dedication to the game have not gone entirely unrecognized nor unrewarded. No, he never saw the kind of money he might have gained in another time, but he's got an army of friends and . admirers. He's been awarded his own place of honor in the Michigan Golf Hall of Fame. And on any sunny summer morning, chances are you'll find him somewhere near the practice tee with a basket of balls waiting to find their way to the green grass that beckons in the distance.

Soon the winds of a new season will carpet this place called Rackham with the rusty brown and yellow hues of the falling maple leaves. For a time, Ben Davis will seek shelter from the harsh elements that visit Michigan each winter.

While others who are more fortunate may take their polished putters and irons south to the fairways and sandtraps below the Mason-Dixon line, Ben will be here at home in Detroit. No, he isn't hibernating, just resting up a little before the crocus and the budding branches of the stately oaks call him back for another lesson at the tee of the game called his life.

Everything's Up in the Air

They fly through the air
with the greatest of ease
as their silent wings search
for an uplifting breeze.

It is freedom they seek
from the earth's surly bonds
The freedom to soar over
trees, hills and ponds.

It's the freedom to just be alone in the sky,
to share the same space
where the bald eagle flies.

"We're going to stick close to home," says the pilot as we
float into the gray-blue clouds. "There's not a lot of lift up
here today, so we'll circle around and just enjoy the view."

It is the solace and thrill
which brings us up here,
to these dizzying heights
that most of us fear.

Three-thousand, four-thousand
the altimeter reads...
The rising warm air
providing all that we need.

With no engine to sputter
and no fuel in her hold,
It's the purest form of flying
which thrills us, we're told.

"It's just freedom," the big man in the floral shirt tries
to explain. "It's the purest form of freedom I could possibly
know."

They're an unusual bunch
that come to this place.
It's just a modest grass field
in a wide open space.

No, you can't find this airport
on any map that you own.
It's in Livingston County
not too far from your home.

Each weekend they gather
to talk and to fly…
and to keep the place running,
or to teach others to try.

They all chipped in some money
to buy the grass field,
'cause airports aren't cheap
and this was a good deal.

See, there's no place on the runways
anywhere else anymore…
for those who love gliders
and have that passion to soar.

So the Sand Hill Soaring Club
took matters in hand,
with their feet on the ground,
they went out and bought their own land.

Now they can fly every day
when the weather permits,
and their flights flown in fancy
can't give neighbors the fits.

Why do it you say?
How much fun can it be?
Perhaps it's like winning the lottery
and you can take that from me.

It's like nothing you've tried
either on the land or the seas,
It's just you and the heavens...
so what more can there be?

It must get in the blood
and take over the heart,
'cause for the pilots of gliders
it's what sets them apart.

Eberhand Guyer's an instructor
we're told...
sharing the passion of soaring
with both the young and the old.

Yup, he's eighty years young
but still in control
of the ship in the wind
which once stole his soul.

"I learned to soar in Germany, when I was very young,"
he says in his lyrical accent. "You know, they were going
to use them in the War. They are a wonderful thing. With a
glider you just fly into the wind...so peaceful, yah?"

Chuck Franklin's another one
who spends time in the sky.
He's from a family of pilots
who taught him to fly.

Years ago, they built gliders
the Michigan way…
so they were born in Chuck's genes
and they're in him to stay.

"It's still a thrill to go up," says the man behind the aviator glasses and pilot's white shirt. "You don't have all that engine noise and other things to worry about. It's quiet. All you hear is the wind beneath the wings."

Dave Beebe's a pilot,
yes, he's a club member too.
Which means soar when you can
and mow the lawn when you're through.

There are tow lines to fix,
there's a winch to repair…
Well, if you're gonna soar with the eagles,
a few chores do seem fair.

"You can be a doctor or a lawyer or the head of a big company, but you leave that out there at the road when you come here," says the big man who was turning a propeller on the tow plane a few minutes before. "Everybody's equal here when there's work to be done."

Now if some weekend
you're in search of something to do,
the gang out at Sandhill
will be there waiting for you.

They'll show you their aircraft
and they'll speak of the joys
of soaring in silence
well beyond the earth's noise.

If you're daring and bold
they'll take you up for a ride,
they'll show you the ropes
and the green countryside.

You'll soar in the wind
with the sun at your side
and you'll know what it's like
finding peace when you glide.

There's just nothing quite like it
and you can take that from me,
because it's the closest to heaven
you're ever likely to be.

The Piano Man

His hands easily travel at the speed of sound. His fingers move almost at the speed of light, touching down softly, briefly, to stroke an ivory or an ebony key before speeding on to another.

In milliseconds, the streaking hands create a rhapsody in rhythm and cascading notes which instantly separate the basics of Beethoven from the bawdy barrelhouse of boogie woogie.

It is the music of the jazz age and the juke joint. A raucous, rollicking excursion into the yellowed pages of our past, drenched in the aromas of cheap whisky, stale cigars, and dime-store perfume. It is the music of a thousand seamless nights bathed in the relentless joy to be found in the pulsating strings of the hammered eighty-eights. It's boogie, and a quiet man named Bob Seeley is its acknowledged master.

"I like to play boogie fast and loud and furious," the master says in studied nonchalance. He speaks as if it were a simple accomplishment, but anyone who has suffered through a first lesson at the piano knows better.

Music, like the societies it so well serves, is evolutionary. It is in constant change to reflect in sound the invisible auras of the day and time in which it is played. So it is that boogie woogie was born of simpler times and simpler tastes.

"Classic boogie woogie comes right out of the blues," he eagerly explains. "Most people think of the blues as sad music, but I call boogie the happy blues."

Some would argue that the music came out of hard times, hard times that some chose then, and even now, to forget. But the notes have survived to linger in a mirrored tribute to those days when the players sat on well-worn stools, hands flying, feet stomping, in a passing moment that would ultimately create a purely unique American form of music.

Almost three-quarters of a century beyond its heyday, Bob Seeley is the keeper of the flame. His hands and unfettered fingers are keeping the heart, soul, and tradition of boogie woogie piano alive. It is the true rhythm of his life and every day he holds its long and almost forgotten history in his hands.

The keyboard is never far from his wandering hands, whether he's in a European concert hall, or headlining a New York jazz festival, or where he feels most at home, behind the piano bar at Charley's Crab in the Hilton Hotel in Troy, Michigan. It is in the piano bar, where it seems he has played forever, that the music comes alive. Seated quietly on a familiar bench, he plays the night away as guests stare in wonder, feet tapping to the feverish rhythms that the piano man pounds out as the cocktail chatter collides and coalesces with the music from another time.

For a few hours in the night, the music of the forgotten

masters of the boogie art is made fresh again, young again, as it races through the veins, sprinting across the keys, leaping the generations in the delicious mix of alcohol, cigarette smoke, and restaurant food.

"This all began for me when a friend of mine who was a banjo player—he did those sing-a-longs in a bar in California—well, he called me, because he needed a piano player, and I wasn't doing much, so off I went to California. I played boogie in between the sing-a-longs and the crowds seemed to like it. So here I am," he says with a trademark smile that comes from telling the tale too many times.

Like too many others who have chosen to labor in the obscure shadows which linger well beyond pop music's mainstream, Bob Seeley's remarkable talent has gone largely unheralded. He has no big-time recording contract, no dates to appear on *The Tonight Show*, just another trip to Europe next month where the art of boogie woogie hasn't been forgotten or ignored.

His name is already on the posters over there. The tickets to his concert are already being sold. No doubt there will be a huge crowd on hand when the boogie woogie faithful gather in tribute to a true master of America's forgotten music.

"Trust me, you'll never make a killing doing this. You'll never get rich playing this stuff. It's just a passion…that's it, it's just a passion," says the piano man. This time, the smile seems more real. This time, the words are coming from the heart.

Ridin' the Southern Michigan Rails

The rails seem to merge together in that strange distance between here and there, which we have learned to call perspective. Once upon a time, the tracks belonged to the very first railroad west of the Pennsylvania mountains. It was called the Erie and Kalamazoo Railroad. In those days, around 1836, the trains would run between Toledo, Ohio and Adrian, Michigan. The line was extended in 1838 to reach Tecumseh, and then fifteen years later, the trains rumbled all the way into Clinton. By then, it had become known as the Southern Michigan Railroad.

"This is our forty-four-ton locomotive," says the man who will soon put on his conductor's cap and navy vest. "The cars are all basically from the early 1920s." The brief history lesson will have to continue later; the conductor has to climb on board to get ready for the passengers who will be arriving shortly.

The Southern Michigan Railroad has had a lot of names in the past. It was part of the New York Central Line. It was Penn Central for a time. Conrail even claimed it briefly before abandoning it back in 1981. That's when a group of high-school model railroaders got together to resurrect the all-volunteer Southern Michigan Railroad.

"It's a short story," a volunteer named Celia offers. "The history of this train is…we saved it. Now we just take people back to see what it used to be." That explanation out of the way, Celia can get on with the business of selling tickets to ride her train.

It's not everybody that gets a chance to run their own railroad, but in this case, everybody does run their own railroad. It's a dedicated, fervent, serious, and hardworking core of volunteers that keeps the little train on the right tracks during the busy visitor season.

By Amtrak standards, the S.M.R. isn't much of a railroad. But if nostalgia and just plain fun have a price tag, the Southern Michigan Railroad is worth its weight in platinum.

"All Aboooaaarrrrd," the conductor shouts. The cars lurch briefly; the sounds of the huge wheels can be heard almost grinding on the old tracks, and the S.M.R. is once again rolling through the familiar terrain of southern Michigan.

It's a guided tour, of sorts. To the curious, the conductor is happy to point out the points of interest. "We're about to go over the highest bridge on the line. We'll slow down a little so you can get a good picture." The bridge provides enough elevation for even the disinterested children to see the glowing fall colors highlighted in the noontime sun.

"We tell everybody it'll only go about eight miles an hour," another volunteer says under his breath. "But the truth is, we can go up to forty miles an hour. The locomotive can really pull the weight."

The train will not approach anything akin to forty miles an hour on this trip. If it did, the journey would be over before it began.

From June through October, the little train that can, does, albeit slowly. From Clinton to Tecumseh, Michigan, the distance of about four-and-a-half miles, is covered in about an hour's time. But the S.M.R. isn't about getting anywhere; it's all about going somewhere. Maybe it's going in a caboose, or in the open gondola, or in the old Chicago, South Shore, South Bend passenger car with the wavy and often cracked window glass.

"We do have a little problem with some vandalism," says the volunteer conductor. "These cars sit out in the open all the time, and unfortunately the windows make a good target for a kid with a rock." That, of course, is the downside of owning your own railroad.

Back at the ticket window, Celia is ready to wax a little more about the railroad and its history in the hands and hearts of the local townspeople who saved it. "You know, we started out with absolutely nothing but an idea, and it's been—well, we've come a very long way." Without a lot of flowery stuff, that sort of sums it all up rather nicely.

The little train that can spends the winter months resting up. There is maintenance to do: maybe a window to fix, and the diesel locomotive always needs some attention. After a full season, the volunteers who run this railroad can always find something to do.

When June rolls around on the calendar once again, the S.M.R. and its cast of characters will be ready to roll. Round-trip fares will hopefully stay on the reasonable side at ten bucks for adults, eight dollars for seniors, and six for children under the age of twelve. It's not a lot of money to spend a day riding the rails of the first railroad in the state of Michigan.

So, if the magic of a passing train has ever made your heart beat a little faster, isn't it nice to know that the Southern Michigan Railroad is still there to slow you down?

The Picture Book

They say a good picture is worth a thousand words. If that's really true, the next few hundred words are probably superfluous except for the fact they will introduce you to a place you might think you know, and to a man with a camera that you don't know.

The place is Kensington Metropark. Three million of us were visitors there this year, but few of us probably see it in quite the same way as Ted Nelson sees it.

"This is the best time of day to shoot," Ted says, as he watches the morning sun peek over the trees and grassy meadows of his favorite place to begin a day.

How many words are there in a picture? Are there really a thousand, or are there ten thousand, or a million? For a better part of the last twenty years, Ted Nelson has been writing his book about the unique beauty of Kensington Park in the lens of his camera. The shutter has snapped more times than he can estimate, but the countless hours and rolls of film have been winnowed down to ninety-four still photographs that may well contain the entire English language. It's a book born from the heart—Ted's heart, and that of Kensington Park.

"It's just nice to come out here, to have a fresh look at everything. It's different every day and in every season." Ted Nelson is a man of few words and why not? After all, his pictures say so much in silence.

Perhaps it was his thirty years as a biology teacher, or maybe it was the simpler times of his youth that taught his eye to see the unrivalled beauty in the little things, the common things of nature. An oak leaf frozen in the grasp of some autumn ice, a cardinal perched for a portrait moment on a frosted branch; they are the little things we think we see, but rarely pause to ponder.

"I just like to wander around the park. I take my time and look for the little things that seem to work on that day. I guess I'd have to say that sunrise is my favorite time."

Ted's beautiful book, without this many words on its pages, has by now found its way onto many coffee tables around Michigan. It rests there until some inquiring eyes are once again drawn to wander among its pages. It is a search quickly rewarded. The reader will stop for a time to ponder the true wonders of the park. The tranquil moments that lie beyond the sandy beaches, the boat-rental concessions, the asphalt bicycle trails meandering along the park's perimeters. It may be the perfect way to visit this sanctuary of the spirit without moving from the comfort of a favorite easy chair.

"I like to think the common places are just as important to us as the Yosemites or Yellowstones," Ted muses in his quiet way. "Kensington offers us the same chance to observe the real beauty of the world around us, only it's a much shorter drive to get there."

For some, Ted Nelson's larger-than-life book will just be a quick read. It will be little more than a big picture book to be scanned and placed back upon the tabletop that stretches in front of the couch. Too bad for them, for they're not hearing the unspoken words that rest on every page. There are enough of those words to last most of us into yet another millennium.

"As I wrote in the introduction of the book," the author says, "I quote a friend who once told me, 'When I'm in nature all alone, I'm as close to God as I can get.'"

Ted Nelson has helped all of us to get there.

Gen. George Armstrong Custer

He unwillingly stepped across the boundary of immortality on June 25, 1876 on a grassy knoll along the rolling banks of the Little Big Horn River. George Armstrong Custer, the flamboyant, fearless Indian fighter, perished in an anguished moment of military miscalculation. In death, he mystically became the stuff of legend, an icon of the old west, his place in history ironically secured by his adversary's own brutal hand.

As he lay bloodied on that now-cherished ground, could he have imagined that more than a century later he might dress again before a bedroom mirror, or that his signature red scarf would once again encircle his collar, or that his brass buttons would gleam again against the midnight backdrop of his cavalry blues, that he would don his hat to once again regale the curious about his exploits on the vast western plains?

Could he have imagined that he would come to life again as a man named Steve Alexander?

"I don't know what to tell you, other than this just feels

right." The words roll off the tongue with assurance and confidence. They belong to a man who bears a striking resemblance to the martyred hero of the west. His strawberry locks drape loosely over the ears, down across the nape of the neck, and spill onto his shoulders. His facial features are dominated by a walrus moustache that covers the top lip and extends down along the corners of the mouth which are locked in a serious dance with the blue eyes that almost smile beyond the protruding nose. My God, he actually does look like Custer.

"Sometimes I think it's not really an act; it's just natural, it's not me trying to be Custer, it just is…it's just being." It is a hard thing to explain. Steve Alexander really doesn't think he's George Custer, but he is, or he might as well be.

Steve was not born in Ohio like Custer. He was born in Jackson, Michigan. That's a long way from the Little Big Horn, but not far from Monroe, Michigan—a southern border city known perhaps as much for the La-Z-Boy chair company as the adopted home of General George A. Custer.

It was in Monroe that the golden-haired warrior married his beloved "Libby," Elizabeth Clift Bacon, and where the newlyweds spent what they often deemed were the happiest days of their turbulent lives. So too, it was in Monroe that Steve Alexander found his "Libby"—his wife Sandy, and where the two now live happily, in the Custers' actual home.

Steve has been proclaimed the foremost Custer living historian in the U.S. by both the Michigan and Ohio legislatures. Much of his discretionary time is taken up each year portraying his boyhood hero in museums, on theatre stages, and in various recreations of the time celebrated annually in venues around the country. As one might imagine, assuming the identity of George A. Custer—however personally rewarding—does not pay the kind of bills associated with life in the twenty-first century.

"Fortunately for me," Steve says in an almost reverent tone. "I work for the Monroe County Road Commission, and the work gives me an extra bonus. I get to travel all over the county." Steve continues to explain the personal benefits of the job. "Of course, it's changed a lot since Custer's day, but he would have been familiar with it all growing up as a boy here…and that's neat for me to kind of share that experience." Clearly, even at work, General Custer is still hanging around in Steve's never-idle mind.

Custer's life has become Steve and Sandy's life in many ways. They are living the history themselves. They are walking, talking, breathing textbooks, often mirroring in their own speech patterns the time lost so long ago in the gauzy confines of myth.

As she wanders through the parlor of her home, Sandy likes to point out the signs of the time, as if they need to be highlighted. "A lot of my research books are over there." She points to a shelf across the room where a number of old books stand at attention in single file. "You know, Libby was born and raised here. She lived through the Victorian period." Suddenly the book titles make sense.

Steve and Sandy were able to purchase the Custer home a couple of years ago. From the outside, it scarcely resembles the old photographs that are now safely captured under glass in a wooden frame that rests upon the parlor mantel. They are methodically recreating the place as it might have been when the general and Libby dwelled in it a century ago.

No, they are not possessed by Custer's ghost, nor do they see him on a stairwell, or feel Libby's presence in a darkened corner of the room. They are just indulging their love affair with the sense of Custer's history that lives within their hearts.

"We're very fortunate to be able to live here in this house," Steve says with a smile. "If we can, we want to recreate some semblance of what life must have been like for them back in the 1860s." His thought seems to drift as his gaze turns to the artifacts that draw the eye around the room. There are portraits of Libby, single portraits of the general in round walnut frames, an oil lamp which rests on a crocheted doily on top of a small round end table. These are not period pieces. They are reproductions or treasures spirited from garage sales and flea markets that engender the feeling of another time. It'll be perfect when the stairs are finally painted.

Despite living two lives, lives separated by more than 128 years, George and Steve, and Libby and Sandy, appear to get along remarkably well in this day and age. Thanks to the invention of the electric light, the gas-fired furnace, and indoor plumbing, the Custers and the Alexanders are pretty comfortable with their respective places in history.

"It's funny," Steve says stroking his abundant moustache. "There are things that you know—when you do it right—you're in your niche. Well, this just feels right, so I know I'm in my niche."

For Steve and Sandy, each day is a day spent living in history. It is a history revised, of course, because the Battle of the Little Big Horn is one event which has simply not yet come to pass in their lives…and fortunately, it never will.

The Carousel Man

They have delighted us for generations. They amuse, challenge, and tease us, providing a few minutes of distraction in hard times, while linking us to those wonderfully happy moments in childhood we all seem to miss in the complex passage to maturity.

The mighty gold-leafed carousels, their mirrors flashing in the spinning lights, their eclectic animal menageries frozen in mid-leap, their thundering mechanical music machines belching sounds and rhythms to assault the ear, are the stuff of another age.

They once dotted the American landscape from tiny villages to remote rural farm towns, but as we changed as a people, we left them behind, some to burn, some to just decay, most simply to be abandoned, retired, and forgotten.

"Of all the thousands and thousands of carousels produced in the past one hundred years, only about three percent of them survive today." These are the words of the man who may be the ranking authority on the great carousels in the United States.

Fortunately, there are a few of the wondrous machines still found around the country. Most have been preserved and restored to grace the playgrounds of the rich and famous, or to gleam in the spotlights of museums, their magnificent wooden carving almost alive again thanks to the skilled hands of Tony Orlando.

"I live in a fantasyland every day," says the small man, who greets us in a dark turtleneck that matches his salt-and-pepper hair. There were sixteen factories at the turn of the century producing the figures for the carousels. Each had a distinct style. Just by examining it, I can tell you exactly when a figure was made, where it came from, and most of its history." Tony Orlando is the encyclopedia carouselia.

From his cramped studio in Dearborn Heights, Michigan, he has carved out a worldwide reputation for his precise and historically correct restorations of giant carousel animals. His mind is a treasury vault containing the colors, the contours, the jeweled highlights, and the carving strokes of the master artisans who brought knurled chunks of often-exotic wood to life, in the vertical columns of a whirling merry-go-round.

"I always have to do a lot of research first before I start on a figure," Tony admits. "I want each figure to be historically accurate. If I get a figure that has been sanded down with no paint, I go to the books. I will come as close to the original as humanly possible."

There are very few timelines in Tony Orlando's world. He can't tell a customer just how long it will take him to bring a neglected stallion back to its pristine beginnings. He can't or won't count the hours he will spend sanding, carefully blending paint colors, how long it will take to find—and then glue—the perfect silver jewels that must be replaced on the delicately carved harness that drapes along the horse's muscular frame. It just takes Tony as long as it takes to make it perfect, because the pursuit of perfection is what keeps his heart in that place where it so obviously belongs.

"Every time I finish a figure," the artist patiently explains, "I have taken something that was given up for junk, and brought it back to life again. The names of those great craftsmen and artists who created the figure years ago live on when I'm done with my part of the work."

Forsaking a career in commercial art has probably cost Tony Orlando a lot of money over the years. Even though some of his restored carousel figures have sold for well over six figures, it's not about the money; it's about the past, and about the history he so deliberately has tried to keep fresh in a throwaway world.

It's the art that has drawn him to his studio, the art of masters past, and his art of a master present. It's all about a time which provided children and parents alike with fun through function. It's about a day in childhood that has been recalled in priceless beauty and timeless craftsmanship. It's about a period when the world was a simpler place and we once rode on the back of a gilded circus animal, grasping at the little brass ring beyond our fingertips.

Writin' on the Line

The words, the original thoughts, the scenes themselves do not always flow easily from the hand to the paper. This is, however, the way author Christopher Paul Curtis prefers to write his books. There is no computer, no fancy word processor, not even a typewriter nearby. There is the ever-present yellow legal pad, a steady hand, and the relentless dedication that accompanies the desire to produce something special, something lasting, for young people to read.

At the ripe young age of forty-seven, Chris Curtis finds himself these days in the lofty company of the literati. His first book, *The Watsons Go to Birmingham,* has been widely acclaimed and won numerous prestigious awards. His new book, *Bud, not Buddy*, appears destined for the same kind of success. That's no small feat for a guy who was hanging doors on a Buick at Fisher Body Plant Number One in Flint when he truly became an author.

"You don't have to be a genius to write a book," he says with a chuckle and mile-wide grin. "You just have to do it." Easy for him to say. "Heck, I still wake up and pinch myself to remember that I don't have to get up and go to the line every day."

Life has become something of a whirlwind lately for Chris. With the huge success of his first book, he's now in demand for personal appearances, book signings, and endless promotional tours that seem to stretch across the entire country at times. Chris Curtis isn't into all of that, however. He would much rather be at a table writing another book for African-American kids to read, to relate to. This is at the heart of the matter for the assembly worker turned writer.

This was no overnight success trip for Christopher. He would be the first one to tell you that without the support of his wife Kaysandra, who is a licensed practical nurse, his dream to write books might have remained just that—a dream never to be realized.

Fortunately, Kaysandra believed in those handwritten words on the yellow sheets of paper, as well as the man who was so laboriously putting them there, and she finally was able to push him over the career edge. Kaysandra told Chris it was time to walk off the line and give his writing a chance. It wasn't too long before his days at the Buick plant were behind him for good.

"I'd just go to the library with no plan in my head. I'd sit there with no story in mind, I'd just start writing something down. Then suddenly a ten-year-old's voice came to me and from that point on it became easy." Chris still writes his books the same way. The voice of a child suddenly comes to him and he's off and running.

Chris has moved in the years since he left the assembly line. He and Kaysandra live in Windsor, Ontario on a quiet tree-lined street. His routine has changed too. He picks up daughter Cydney from school each day, maybe on the way home from the library where he still goes to get in touch with the little voices that propel his hands across the paper. It's pretty normal family stuff for a celebrated author.

Sure, Chris can still find time to shoot a few hoops around the backyard net. He still finds time to get in the groove of some old Motown records by his favorite singers. But it's the writing that pumps his heart and drives the pure soul of the man who wants every kid to have the chance to read.

"Books have always made a real difference in my life," the author recalls. "While there weren't a lot of books for me as an African American to read, I still loved books, books with good stories. Now, that's what I'm trying to do, write good stories. I think the factory gave me the discipline necessary to be a writer."

Some would probably say there is a fairytale quality to the personal journey of Christopher Curtis, the storyteller from Buick City who managed to write on the line during his breaks. The story of the not-so-old author who suddenly climbed to the top of the children's bestseller lists with a book that came from the voice of the little boy that lives somewhere very close to his heart.

But it's not a fairy tale at all—it's the real thing—and after all, true stories almost always seem to be the best ones anyway, don't you think?

"It's very gratifying to hear kids tell me how important my books are to them." Chris says modestly. "It makes me feel so good and it's such a long way from hanging a door on a Buick."

So Long to the Soup

As local landmarks disappear around Detroit these days, the little brick building at the corner of Franklin and Orleans is pretty small potatoes in the great scheme of things. Its passing, however, is worth a moment or two of reflection because it has held such a special place in the hearts of so many. Not just Detroiters, but in the national community of traveling musicians who, for decades, have come to its doors knowing that an audience at the Soup Kitchen Saloon would appreciate why they came.

For years, a simple sign on Jefferson Avenue has pointed the way to the corner that has been Detroit's official "Home of the Blues."

"It's the real thing," says longtime owner Brian McDonald. "It's not just one more of those bars that decided to play a particular kind of music to attract customers. There has been a real effort here to promote and to play the blues when it was not a very popular thing to do."

We now have to speak of the Soup Kitchen Saloon in the past tense. Yes, its name has confused some at times. There is the Capuchin Soup Kitchen a few blocks away, but it's a charity where daily meals are dispensed to the displaced and hungry. Here we speak of the purveyor of good spirit, in the form of both alcohol and quality entertainment.

For the past few years, the Soup's life expectancy had to be measured in months or weeks. Its future had been sealed by the leaders of the city who had determined that it was in everyone's best interest to run a lot of little businesses out of town so some very big casino businesses could take over and develop the area.

The dark gambling cloud that hovered over the few blocks that had become known as Rivertown had a serious choking effect on almost everyone who had taken the chance over the years to open their doors in a not-so-nice part of town. Some stayed, some left, but Rivertown was starting to thrive until the day the casinos came to town.

So it was that on a Saturday night, without fanfare, without a chance to say goodbye, without a last bowl of beef and barley soup, the Soup Kitchen Saloon was suddenly gone. The doors closed for a final time to await the wrecker's ball and the grand gambling palace that was scheduled to overwhelm the little corner at Franklin and Orleans.

"It's a very odd feeling," Brian McDonald tries to explain. "I feel like I'm being forced into early retirement. I'm not sure what to make of it all quite yet. After twenty-five years of being in the middle of things, it's very unusual to be on the sidelines. All I can say after the last sixty days of uncertainty is I just have a very odd feeling."

Brian McDonald gave the blues a place to call home in Detroit in the mid-seventies. On a tiny stage, in a cramped room, the legends of the music sang and played, sharing an intimacy with their fans lost long ago in the vastness of public arenas and impersonal concert halls. At the Soup Kitchen, it wasn't just a show for the audience; it was a personal experience to be shared on a creaky barroom chair, complete with plastic tablecloth and flickering red citronella candlelight.

"The idea that people could come here—all kinds of people—I think really helped the music reach out to everyone," the proprietor says a bit wistfully. "You know, the music is far more popular today."

The pictures, staggered so perfectly along the yellowed smoke-stained walls, are graphic reminders of the history held in the backroom's past. The aged brick, chipped in so many places, hint that this was the oldest continuously operating bar within the city's limits.

In its heyday, it was a sailor's hangout, a tawdry house of ill repute, and a haven for the prohibition-era Purple Gang. Its varied history seems to all but ooze from the wooden planks of the scuffed, worn floor behind the ancient bar. Alas, that is the past and now it's hard to see anything but a spinning roulette wheel in its future.

"I guess I wish if they're gonna do it…well, I just wish they'd do it and get it over with," the words seem to come a little harder, but they emerge without the bitterness one might expect from an entrepreneur who has had his life unbalanced by the greedy whims of some downtown power brokers.

There is no bitter aftertaste in Brian McDonald's mouth. He knows he has stayed the course at the Soup. He is proud that he managed to survive the tough recessions, survived the crime wave that swept along Jefferson Avenue. Yup, he survived and stayed while others with fancier names and wealthier clientele folded up and headed north of Eight Mile Road to the safety of the suburbs. The Soup Kitchen hung on and the people came to Brian's home of the blues.

The people came for almost thirty years, packing the tables in the crowded back room where legends of the music like Albert Collins, Little Sonny, Fenton Robinson, Sippie Wallace, Willie Warren, and so many others brought the night and the music to life, and the blues to its righteous Motor City home. For a hundred months, it was a boundless synergy of time and place, altered only by the dreaded nightly shout of "last call" on the house PA system. Those words became the only means to achieve the reluctant surrender of an evening well spent among strangers who have become friends in the fraternity of the music.

"This place brought people from miles away," McDonald remembers. "There was a buzz out there among the musicians. They all wanted to come and play the Soup Kitchen. And the people wanted to come and hear them and applaud the fact that they had come to our town to be part of us."

Perhaps it was the best thing to do, to just close the doors up one night, to leave the tippy tables in place, the bottles in silence behind the high bar, the glasses still hanging from their stems in the overhead racks, and the pictures—all of those pictures—still resting against the walls. With the simple turn of a key, the Soup Kitchen became a museum, a home without a home, a place without a place to be, trapped between the memories of a rich past and the haunting uncertainties of a future yet to be conceived.

Brian McDonald stands for a last time behind the bulky bar that seems to almost divide the past from the present.

The beer taps still glisten as though they had just been polished to instantly display the bold brand name sealed beneath the acrylic veneer. The glasses sparkle and shine in a rainbowed reflection of the light overhead.

"I toughed it out and I'm proud of it," says the man with no present occupation. "I stayed when a lot of people ran, and I'm glad I did. There's never been a regret for me. I've always felt it was not only my place in life, but my city, my neighborhood…and I never questioned being here every day. It's just been the place where I belonged."

For a long time, people still came to the closed doors. Apparently, word of the Soup Kitchen's passing didn't pass very well among the faithful patrons. They came to the black doors under the green awning to briefly peer through the glass into the darkened entrance lobby. Perhaps they came to rekindle a memory, or maybe they came to pay their final respects, only to discover that they had come too late.

The lights are now officially out on this little corner of the city's history, and Detroit's once-proud home of the blues is gone.

Note: The gambler's paradise, scheduled to be built upon the site of the Soup Kitchen, never came to pass. Plans for the huge casinos along the Detroit riverfront were eventually scuttled and deemed to be economically unsound. The area called "Rivertown" is now owned by the city and lays blighted and abandoned. The Soup Kitchen, gutted of its memorabilia at public auction, burned to the ground in the fall of 2003. Brian McDonald moved to Fort Myers, Florida.

Transformations

The Town Cheerleader

"Hey, howya doin'? Great to see you out here today."
His friends like to call him "the Mayor of Belle Isle."
It is an accolade well deserved for a man who decided nearly
twenty years ago it was time to do something special for
the kids of Detroit.

It was natural. After all, a few decades ago, he was a kid
himself, growing up in Detroit. He went to the old Eastern
High School, working long hours after classes in his dad's
neighborhood grocery store. The fact is, Ed Deeb loved his
city then, and he still does, and that's why he went to work
on an idea to bring kids, volunteers, and a community together, on a day called Metro Youth Day in Detroit.

"It was a good thing that happened out of a bad thing,"
the unofficial mayor of the island rushes to explain. "It all
started with some problems between some store owners and
some neighborhood kids that escalated into tensions. There
was a lot of trouble and a shooting. We just knew we had to
do something." His words are chosen carefully because he
wants no misunderstandings. He may rush a lot, but not
when it comes to the important stuff.

131

To make Metro Youth Day happen, Ed had to do some serious shopping. He had to come up with eight hundred pounds of potato chips, ice cream, and cookies. He needed seven hundred pounds of hot dogs, one hundred forty gallons of fruit juice, and nine hundred gallons of soda pop. That's a pretty hefty grocery list by anybody's standards, but that's what Ed needed to play host to about twelve thousand kids on a warm summer day on his island in July.

Undaunted by the enormity of the task, Ed Deeb prevailed. "The bottom line was clear. We wanted these kids to get the message. We just wanted them to know that somebody in their community cared about them." A lot of kids soon learned the meaning of his earnest and honest words.

As head of the Michigan Food and Beverage Association, the "mayor" didn't have to look very far for help. Over nine hundred volunteers quickly signed on to provide the treats and help pass them out. It was no small feat and it caught the eye of then-President George H. W. Bush, who recognized Youth Day with his prestigious Point of Light Award.

"The great part is," Ed Deeb says, "we've gone way beyond the games and all the fun things. Now we're giving scholarships to kids to go to college. I'll tell you it warms my heart every time I see one of those kids receive that chance of an education."

While Metro Youth Day and Ed Deeb's name are virtually synonymous, his heart is found in a lot of other city spots as well. Eastern Market is the latest to sample the Deeb touch. When the troubled eastside landmark needed a hand, it turned to Deeb.

"No question, there was a lot of frustration in the Market." From kids on Belle Isle to an aging city centerpiece, he quickly shifts focus, reorienting priorities. Each task, however, is attacked with the same gusto. "The merchants in the market, you know many of them have been there for generations…well, they weren't able to communicate their troubles, their concerns properly to City Hall. That's where I come in."

The revitalization of the Eastern Market area is a passion for Ed these days. He knows the history well. He was there often as a Detroit kid who worked in the grocery business. He knows about the hard times and the few good times. He also happens to know most of the movers and shakers in Motown and Lansing on a first-name basis. Ed Deeb is in the business of getting things done, or making the wrongs right.

"It's about getting people wound up. Ya gotta get 'em going. Ya gotta get 'em energized to do something positive, to do something that's gonna be good for everybody in the end. They just have to see that part of it, and then they'll do something." The words come with an almost religious passion when Ed gets going. He's just that way.

Maybe it's the perpetual smile on Ed's face that does the work for him. Maybe that's why no one seems to be able to say "no" to him when he's on one of his many missions. Perhaps he's really part city ambassador and part seasoned diplomat. They are roles he has played with success in the Arab-American community and the community at large.

One thing is certain: Ed Deeb, the kid from the east side who went to Michigan State on a music scholarship, will never toot his own horn about his accomplishments. That's just not his style, but he must be considered the captain of his city's unofficial—and still unappointed—cheerleading squad.

"I love this city…I just want to see it all work," the busy man quickly says, as he hurries away to his next appointment. Every urban center needs a cheerleader these days, and Detroit's lucky to have one with a heart the size of Ed Deeb's.

Bear Tracks in Her Heart

Perhaps it's in their gentle faces, or in the fuzzy warmth that is sure to come with the hug for which they seem to beg. Perhaps they speak to us, without words, of the days when we were children. Maybe they speak silently of the nights they shared our pillows, or the year we knew we had grown too old to play together anymore. No matter.

In a world wearied by the complex, they still speak to us in the simplest terms. They speak individually, as if they really cared, and perhaps that's why Paula Spencer has to make them for us.

"I always tell people, look at the bear and the bear will make you smile; the bear will make you think happy thoughts." It is the simple philosophy of this everybody's grandma. The eyes twinkle above the line in the bifocals that have shifted ever so slightly down toward the bridge of the nose. Her hands show the passing of time and the hours spent in her special calling.

Paula makes bears, teddy bears of character. Her first one was born about five hundred bears ago, following the

135

widow's rebound from the appalling prospects of breast cancer. Time was hanging too heavily at her fingertips, so with the encouragement of her sister, Leona, she put her hands and fingers to work. She made a bear. And then she made another. Paula started making bears to make other people feel better. She called them her "hope" bears.

"I was very lucky," Paula says. "I didn't have to have chemo, and when I came out of it, I felt like there's something...there's some reason I'm still here." The recollection is difficult, but flows with the honesty which comes in the aftermath of tragedy averted. "That was when the bears came along...and they filled a very great void in my life."

No two of Paula's bears are ever alike. They just can't be. Each must have its own flavor, its own personality, and its own character. Some, the ones she calls her "memory" bears, have become treasures to those who now hold them. In time they become living reminders of a lost loved one. You see, Paula makes her special "memory" bears from a remnant of life: perhaps a coat, a piece of a dress, or a swatch of cloth saved from a blanket or a flannel shirt that once belonged to someone who has left this world, but who left behind something far more lasting than a fading memory.

"I think this is wool," she says grasping the cloth between two fingers and rubbing it, as if the answer is to be found in the mere touching. "I had this one lady that I made a bear for...she just cried and cried when she saw it. It was made out of her father's favorite robe. She just cried." That's why she calls them her "memory" bears.

When she's not hunched over her sewing table creating one of her special bears, Paula can usually be found doing volunteer work with the local hospice organization near her home in Alger, Michigan. If she's not there, then she's probably visiting or sewing with her sister, Leona, who is also a widow. In one of those strange twists of fate, the sisters married two brothers, so they have always shared the same last name in life.

Leona Spencer is the quiet one as the two sit by the Singer machines, silhouetted in their work by the glaring daylight that pours into the room. The work of bear making always seems to go more slowly at Leona's house.

"I'll be lucky if I can get the legs sewn on this one today," Paula observes, almost under her breath. Leona, not an arm's length away, offers up a thought. "Well, no poked fingers yet, that's good." The sewing continues and so does the conversation and that's what makes the business of creating bears a little less productive in Leona's room.

Although she could probably turn her "hope" bears and "memory" bears into a thriving business, Paula won't. She won't because they are far too personal to her. She believes they are each made with a special mission. They are made to produce a smile. They are made to renew hope. They are made to recall a cherished memory.

"Sometimes I walk with my dog and I say thank you to God for giving me this bear talent. It's a talent I never knew I had." Paula seems lost in her own memory for a moment. With a much wider smile and a chuckle, she concludes, "I'm sixty-nine years old and I start making bears..." The sentence hangs where it was left, and the head shakes slowly from side to side. It's just Paula's silent way of saying she'll never understand how or why she has become the "bear lady" of Alger, Michigan.

The Making of a Monument

The images of the scratched film still haunt us, and they should, for time has not healed the wounds, nor has it paid the price for the young lives that were stolen from America's homes.

Time has merely tried to hide the images, obscure them, or even worse, revise them. For those of us of the Vietnam generation, much time has passed, but the hands on that clock still remain frozen at the hour of our betrayal.

The angst was supposed to end with the abandonment of Saigon, or beside the flag-draped coffin of the last American to fall. Yes, the shooting finally stopped in the most divisive conflict of the twentieth century, but the bleeding didn't and hasn't. That's why a dedicated high-school teacher from suburban Fraser can't let it go, can't allow us to forget the names of 2,649 sons and daughters from eighty-three different Michigan counties.

"Per capita, Michigan paid a very high price for that war," says the man in the blue-checked shirt. He sits erect, with an almost military posture, as he continues. "If you saw all the names listed, it would look like a small-town phone book.

It doesn't sound like a lot when we talk these days about millions and trillions of dollars, but when you see that many names on a wall—well, it'll overwhelm you."

Mike Sand has spent too many years now trying to convince the rest of us the lives of those 2,649 people mattered, that they need to be remembered, honored, and preserved for future generations. Mike has spent more time on the Michigan Vietnam Monument Commission than he did repairing our fighter planes and bombers at the clandestine airbase in Thailand where he was stationed during the war. Simply put, Mike hasn't forgotten what time might one day let us all forget.

"I came home and tried to get on with my life," he says stoically. "I spent ten years in the 'bush'—or what we call the closet—not letting anyone know I'd served in Vietnam." His words grow darker. "One day, I met this fellow who was wearing a hat that read: 'Vietnam Veterans of America.' I inquired about it, and he said, 'Man we've got to get together, we've got to find each other because we all came home alone.'" The memory is still too fresh in Mike Sand's mind.

In his long battle to bring a lasting Vietnam memorial to the state of Michigan, there have been many advances, and more than a few retreats. The site of the monument is now secure, however, and all of the plans have been drawn up and approved. A lot of money has been raised along the way, just not enough to push the dream off the architect's paper and into the eternity of the Capitol grounds.

As he pores over the black-and-white sketches on the drawing table, he explains the symbolism behind each of the pen strokes. "We call it tension and strength," Mike says softly. The renderings display a walking plaza with vertical columns separated by an overhead wire that appears to stretch the length of the site. "I think it's very powerful." It is.

The idea of a Michigan monument strangely has its detractors. There are those who think the names carved into the black granite wall in Washington should be enough to satisfy the need to recall the price of conflict. There are those who seem to think the pain of a useless war should be buried in the same graves as those who fought it. Fortunately, there are people like Mike Sand who know better. He knows the monument is for the living, and for those yet to live.

"If we can get enough people to come on board with us, and we can raise the money, we can get a shovel in the ground." At this point in time, Mike says the project needs another million or so dollars to spring it from the paper. "We'd like to build it right along with the new Hall of Justice building behind the Capitol. It would be so beautiful, and so ironic; it would be so wonderful to say that justice has finally come home." He raises his arms skyward and glances to the heavens.

Over four decades after the nightmare of Vietnam, it is still unreconciled for many. It still hides behind the eyes of those who were there. It still lingers in the hearts of those who refused to serve. It still resides in the souls of those who sought and squandered deferments. It still haunts those who hid in the shadows of the other, safer branches of the service.

That's why Mike Sand and the other 450,000 Michigan survivors of Vietnam want and deserve this lasting tribute.

"It will give special meaning to all of us," he says, although he's said it a thousand times before. "There are about 450,000 of us Vietnam vets in Michigan, and you can imagine, each person that served has about eight people in their family that were touched, in some way, by the war. Those are the people who need this monument."

Note: After years of planning and fundraising, the dream of a Vietnam Memorial became a reality on November 11, 2001. On hallowed ground behind the Capitol building, the author was honored to serve as the Master of Ceremonies at the official dedication ceremony. He urges you to visit and spend a few moments in contemplation. You will be glad you did.

Remembering Bill

It began on July 23, 1967. The late Walter Reuther called them "the days of madness"—and surely they were.

Federal troops controlled the streets, forty-three people lay dead, and a once-proud city was left to choke on its broken promises to diversity.

Others tried to analyze what had gone wrong, but Bill Cunningham already knew. Out of the smoke and the lingering shadows of insurrection walked this humble man with what must have seemed, even to him, to be an impossible dream.

Father William Cunningham was a teacher of English at Sacred Heart Seminary when the buildings around him burned and the machine guns blazed on Linwood Avenue, just steps from the confines of his quiet classroom. The bloody fury he witnessed on the streets tore at his very soul.

He simply could not stand still and watch his city die, so he put away his textbooks, followed his conscience, and began his inspired journey to commitment. Where others saw despair, he saw promise. Where others saw blight, he saw rebirth. Where others saw only hopelessness, he saw hope—and less than eight months after the final flame of the rebellion had been extinguished, Focus: HOPE was born.

In an old factory building on Oakman Boulevard, Focus: HOPE began its mission modestly. It first opened a food distribution center where surplus government commodities were given to the poor in an atmosphere of dignity and personal caring. The hungry were to be fed, and soon the naked would be clothed.

It didn't take long. Hundreds, then thousands of people of good will quickly joined the pied piper of justice and righteousness in his unique urban crusade. There would be precious little help from Washington in those early days, but the messenger of Focus: HOPE was indefatigable. No one could hide from his relentless Irish smile, his unrelenting human spirit, his passionate personal mission.

Father Bill Cunningham could beg a million from a miser just as easily as he could cajole a pledge from a pauper. No one could say "no" to him—but if somehow they did, they did so with the knowledge that he would be back to work them over again, and the next time he would appear with an even more compelling plea.

He defied the political climate of the time. As the decade of the 1960s was closing, America had murdered its heroes, tried to suppress dissent on its college campuses, and Nixon, Agnew, and George Wallace had turned the political label "Liberal" into a dirty word. The momentum of the civil rights struggle was being blunted. The code words "law and order" had replaced "justice and equality" in the official vocabulary of the Washington establishment, yet quietly, from the sanctuary of his small inner-city parish, the irrepressible priest was pressing on.

By 1976, the days of the great charismatic marches had clearly faded, but the people still came to march with Father Cunningham and the people of Focus: HOPE. They came in the name of brotherhood, social justice and community caring. They came every October by the hundreds. They came year after year after year. Twenty years later, on October 13, 1996 they came again just weeks after Father Cunningham had emotionally revealed that he had been stricken with a deadly form of cancer.

Pale, thin, and obviously wearied from his infection and therapy, he retraced a few of the countless steps that seemed to symbolize the path of his singular vision for almost thirty years.

Once again he was among friends on that October day. He walked with the mayor, the cardinal of his church, his business allies, the dreamers, the doers, the believers, the caregivers, the caretakers, the would-bes, the hope-to-bes, and of course, the poor and the disabled for whom he had toiled so long and so fruitfully. All had come that day to be with him on what would be his final walk for justice.

What had begun in 1967 as a simple social experiment had, in the ensuing decades, matured well beyond slogans, labels, and lofty liberal mission statements. Focus: HOPE was no longer simple, nor could it be considered experimental, for it had succeeded so boldly where so many others, even those with the best of intentions, had managed to fail.

Somehow, this gentle cleric, whose soaring spirit was never trapped in the formal vestments of his faith, had fashioned a miracle. He had machined a miracle, really. A miracle of modern technology had been honed with castoff tools and then secured in some long empty buildings simply abandoned in an accountant's tax write-off plan. The relics of the city's manufacturing past had been resurrected and refurbished to once again teach and feed another generation.

Father Cunningham knew how to make a marriage work, too. He married rich to poor, new to old, enemy to friend. He managed to bond the public sector to the private, government to business, old to young, teacher to student, white to black, black to white, all in a common purpose of hope in, and for, the future.

In the end, cancer has done what nothing else could. It has silenced the messenger of Focus: HOPE. His message, however, will continue to resound in the lives of those families who once were hungry, or in the memory of a child who needed shoes, or in the gratitude of a troubled teen who was given a chance to learn a skill and then to earn a living wage in the dignity of the workplace.

When this city which he loved so well finally completes its long journey back to life, as it surely will, the citizens of the new Detroit will owe an unpayable debt to this humble champion of the people. My friend Bill would never have dreamed it, but perhaps some time in this new century, or beyond, the official number of saints in the Roman Catholic Church will increase by one.

And why not? His miracles are well documented.

Hec's Bar

Sixty-five years are now gone. No one ever came to write one of those fancy reviews about the place in the newspaper. Take a look around, and the sixty-five years show. The tiles on the floor exhibit clear signs of excessive footwear. The dark, paneled walls were probably a lot lighter once upon a time. The re-upholstered vinyl chairs are due for another re-upholstering. The signs, even the photographs over the cash register, send the senses proof of the times past. They have been stained almost opaque by a zillion smoldering cigarettes. Even with a Michigan head cold, you know what this place smells like!

The clack of a cue ball colliding on a green felt table is the only thing heard over the din of *sotto voce* conversation. Almost everybody knows everybody else in the place. It is a place where the spirit flows freely; if it weren't for the hard stuff, it might as well be a fellowship hour in the church annex.

The talk at this noon hour, however, is not about things ecclesiastical, but of things more earthly and pedestrian. On this day in September, the talk is about the last lunch at Hec's Bar.

There is a mixture of smiles among the faithful who sit along the rolled edge of the well-worn bar. They glance at each other. They gaze blankly into the glass in front of them with the flattening white head of draft beer. The ashtrays host more than a few spent butts, and several fresh ones that send a swirl of light white smoke into the waiting ceiling tiles. It's a still life at the end of life.

"I don't know what I'm gonna do," says one weary patron, contemplating the change in his routine that has become ritual rather than planned repetition. "I dunno, maybe I'll have to start bringing my lunch to work, but where the hell am I gonna eat it?" No one along the bar seems to have an answer.

Another beer drinker, two cigarettes down, says un-equivocally, "This sucks." The direct statement appears to satisfy all and the matter is concluded in conversation for the moment.

The history of Hec's Bar is pretty familiar on the east side. It opened up as a corner speakeasy in the Purple Gang era. The bar then flourished legally in the post-Depression years. It survived the big wars and the little ones. It survived the plant closings in the neighborhood; it even survived the blight that claimed so many of the buildings down the block. It survived the good times and bad, but paradoxically it won't survive the city's own imperfect renaissance.

Hec's Bar has to make way for progress. The building has been sold off to a fast food chain, so a family business built on burgers and beer for three generations will yield to a drive-in window and a synthetic voice which will say "Welcome to White Castle. May I take your order?"

A fresh glass of draft Stroh's prompts another observation for customer number five at the bar. "You know, I've got it right in my will; I've put the money aside and everything. We was gonna have my wake in here. All my friends were gonna come and give me a proper send off. Now what the hell am I gonna do? This is my place, this is my sorry seat." Once again, no answer comes down or across the soggy coasters which stretch into the infinity of the darkened end of the bar.

It's introduction time at Hec's for those who were never able, or for their own reasons, chose not to venture into the place. It began with the founder, Hec Van Maele, sixty-five years ago. Hec's son, Norman, came along awhile back to take over the daily chores, then Norman's son, Bob, picked up the torch in the long family tradition. So behind the bar, for three generations, there has been a Van Maele doling out the spirits. Little did Bob know that he would suddenly become the last in the line of distinguished barkeepers.

"I should tell you about my mom," Bob tells the stranger who has come to say farewell. "Her name is Rose. She came in here with some girlfriends to do a little celebrating one night, and she spotted my dad working behind the bar. She says, right then she knew—and, well, it wasn't long after they were married and she started working in here too."

The story of Hec's Bar is not just about the people. There's a black cat that seems to always be asleep down at the end of the long bar. His name is "Midnight." The cat arrived on a winter's evening in the arms of a cop who felt sorry for it wandering around in the cold in the alleyway out back. Black cats are supposed to be unlucky, but not old Midnight. He knew he had found a home nine years ago, and he has never been out the door since.

The back room of Hec's Bar is Sandy's territory. She's Bob's wife, and knows a thing or two about how to grill a burger and time a load of French fries to perfection. Don't call her the cook; she doesn't care much for that description of her duties.

It's been a family thing for a lot of years, so it's hard to sum up all the feelings when the widest door in your life is suddenly closing shut. Bob has tried to sort the emotions out. So have Sandy, Rose, Dennis, and Joe.

"It's difficult," Bob says with the reluctance which attends any life-altering experience. "There are some good things about it. We've never really had time to do much traveling, or had any real vacations, so we're looking forward to that, I guess. It's hard to see the place go, though. I'll tell ya, if these walls could talk, they'd tell ya some good stories."

Those walls would probably tell of sixty-four New Year's Eve parties, a hundred birthdays celebrated in the vinyl chairs, and the gallons of beer consumed by the winning and losing ball teams supported by the owners of Hec's Bar. The walls would tell of the ten thousand life stories poured freely over the varnished bar in earnest passion by a hundred regular patrons. The walls would remember nights that were too long, and days that were too short. They would speak of arguments and profanities, of hugs and kisses, of noise and silence, of years, days, and minutes.

There simply isn't time to tell all the stories of Hec's Bar. By now it's gone, and with it the walls that now shall never speak.

"Officer Down..."

It was another one of those all-too-many nights which have brought shame to our city. It was another one of those nights which have brought fear to our streets and bars to our windows. It was one of those nights when gunfire rattles beyond a child's sleep. Its sound stirs the curious and sharply signals rage, pain, and all too often, the abrupt conclusion to another's life.

The police radio crackled with the dreadful words no cop wants to hear. "Officer down...Officer down." The response comes instantly: "Did you say officer down? Four thirty-two, I need your location..."

And so it was on an evening in 1995 that Detroit police officer Jerry Philpot surrendered his hopes, his dreams, all those wonderful tomorrows with his wife and daughter, surrendering even his final breath to an AK-47 assault rifle, wielded by a young street-gang member on the city's southwest side. It was the night that altered Diane Philpot's life forever.

"It came across the news, I heard an officer had been

shot—no way did I think it was him." It has been several years, but the memory of May 26, 1995 will always be fresh in Diane's mind. "No way was it him—and then maybe fifteen minutes later a scout car pulled up."

She sits with her legs crossed in an easy chair in her living room. A picture of her husband hugging the couple's daughter rests on the end table next to the chair. Diane Philpot is a small woman, with blonde straight hair that spills across the shoulders and the straps of the denim jumper she favors. "I turned around and I saw Jerry's mother; they were holding her up. I looked at her and I knew. I guess I kind of blanked out and I went into shock."

To the newspapers, TV, and radio, it was another cop homicide. There would be another picture to drape with crepe on the precinct wall, another gathering of uniformed farewells, another teary widow, and another fatherless child. In its very repetition, the trappings of death in the ranks of a city's police force have become too predictable. For Diane Philpot, her policeman's death was a call to find meaning in her suddenly shattered life.

"You don't get over it," she says with emphasis. "There's no closure to it either." Her words now carry a hint of pique and frustration. "You know, a lot of people seem to think you're supposed to grieve for two weeks. After that, you're supposed to just get on with your life as though nothing had happened." Her eyes are now intense as she continues. "Those people haven't been there—they haven't been that close to someone, someone they loved more than anything else in the world."

Diane managed to pick up the pieces of her broken heart, drawing strength from each piece, and, eventually, found both forgiveness and compassion for those who had so casually murdered a good man, the man Diane loved.

"For me, it wasn't that difficult," says the widow. "It was kind of a natural progression for me. I think that God has put that path in front of me to follow."

The path led her back to the very neighborhood where her husband worked and died. As she has done so many times since, Diane Philpot went back to the streets of the southwest side, not in search of her husband's killer, but to find a way to help the kids who live there. She sought a way to reach those young people who often seem beyond reach. Diane simply chose to make a difference, a difference that might prevent another killing someday.

"If they make the decision that they want to get out, to get out of a gang, then I give them a lot of credit for doing that. It takes a lot of guts to do that," she says. "How can I not reach out to them and say okay? I don't want this to ever happen to anybody else. If I don't help these kids, then I feel like I'm letting Jerry down." There is now a lump of emotion in her throat.

The days since that shameful night in 1995 have passed fairly quickly as they tend to do as we gracefully age. Diane's fatherless daughter, Kaitlin, has grown and the questions about Daddy are asked less frequently now. Nonetheless, they still feel the painful loss of Jerry. Through it all, Diane has managed to find peace.

"I want to make a difference now, because I might not be here tomorrow. I've learned that the hard way. But at least, what I do today might make a difference for tomorrow."

These days, Diane is chronically busy. She is a vice president of a police survivors' organization. She is a busy committee member, scratch golfer, churchgoer, dedicated mother, and yes, even a youth gang counselor. All in all, that's a pretty impressive resume from a heart that simply refused to stay broken.

A Day at the Kronk

Somebody once said history is often made in some very strange places. Welcome to one of them. Down a flight of worn stairs, through a locked gray door, one slips into history, boxing history. This is it: the Kronk. A steamy, sweaty, faded recreation center basement that for a fleeting, but golden, time was the penthouse suite of boxing's elite.

It was in the Kronk that a skinny kid from the east side of Detroit met a dedicated teacher from the west side, and the two began a journey to fortune, fame, and failure. They began to live the dream that is almost always born in poverty, raised for a time in uncounted riches, and is usually squandered in the excesses of success.

It's the stuff of life that took a coal miner's son named Emanuel to the top and almost back down to the bottom.

"What happened in my case," the teacher begins to explain, "was that everything, the money, came so fast. I didn't have time to adjust to it. You know, you come out of nowhere with a couple of little boxers and before long, you know, suddenly you're on the top of the world." It's the kind of explanation that has become redundant in its own repetition. It is the sad legacy of too many who have tasted the vintage champagnes of professional boxing.

Emanuel Steward has done things most of us could only imagine. Things we could only do if we hit the lottery or were left a sudden fortune by an unknown relative. He has lived in skyscraper penthouses, hob-nobbed with the stars of Hollywood, traveled the world in limousines and private jets, but after nearly losing it all, he's back. This time, he says, his feet are firmly on the ground, or should we say the mat. This time he's back to where it all began. Emanuel Steward is back at the Kronk.

"I don't know what it is," he says in the clipped words that lace his every conversation. "I can't explain it, except there is a spirit in here. I can't put my finger on it. The boxers just seem to box better in here than anywhere else." The tribute to the place cannot come from a better source.

Emanuel Steward had been gone from the Kronk for a long time, maybe too long, some say. For a time, he became a boxing world mercenary. He was invited into the war camps of the champs and to the practice rings of the pretenders to the thrones. He was the trainer for hire, who had abandoned his roots in Detroit in exchange for the quantum dollars that flowed like good wine from the flamboyant promoters' checkbooks. He was lost until the fading siren of the Kronk called him home again.

"I'm spending most of my time here with the amateur boxers—the young fighters who want the chance to become pros someday. Some of them just like to come in here and train. They'll never be fighters, but they want to be here to learn what it takes. I just like to teach them all," says the acknowledged master of the three-rope ring.

Emanuel says it's all about the kids, kids like Octavio Lara. In the heat of a Kronk afternoon, Emanuel dances with the man-child inside the ropes, staring into the dark eyes as the sweat begins to break across the olive skin of the youngster who jabs away at the leather mitt darting in front of him. In those intense eyes, Emanuel Steward can once again see the future, and perhaps the shadow of a skinny east-side kid named Tommy who won seven different boxing titles.

He isn't skinny anymore. Over in a corner of the Kronk, by a stripe of gold paint, Tommy Hearns is working one of the heavy bags. His biceps recoil with each thrust, his fists hitting just below the "Everlast" trademark on the battered bag. The punches still carry authority, but the snap that once produced so much power seems less fearsome. The champ pauses just briefly in his workout to pay tribute to his mentor.

"You know, Emanuel was a father figure to me." Tommy's words are spoken earnestly, but with the difficulty that comes with too many hits, in too many rounds, in too many fights. "He took me under his wing, and helped to mold me into the person I am today." The honest words speak, perhaps, too honestly about a brutal profession.

The Kronk is, and always will be, a dose of reality. While it is the stuff of dreams for some who come to bask in its historic past, it is nonetheless little more than the true grit on the bottom rung of life's ladder.

As the winter months approach, they will turn the heat back on at the Kronk. The fighters will sweat a little more as they work the bags, lift the weights, and crunch the abdomens on the reclining situp tables. Some will dance the three rounds with Emanuel in the center ring. Some will watch as the former champs, the honored graduates of this special school, try to recreate or even restore what once was in their storied lives. All will be listening, however, for the master has come home to the Kronk. Emanuel Steward has come home to the future in hopes that history can repeat itself in the strange confines of the red and gold place called the Kronk.

"Even though I have traveled all over the world," the master says, "There's just no place like home."

The Angel of 5-North

She has been called an angel on loan from God. Her domain: the institutional hallways of 5-North, the oncology unit of Troy's busy Beaumont Hospital.

She came here about twenty years ago, a young nurse with experience in pediatric and coronary care, not cancer care. She came, in fact, before there was a major cancer treatment center at Troy Beaumont.

There simply was never any doubt in her mind. As a little girl, Carmen Buch just believed she would grow up to be a nurse someday.

"From the time I was twelve years old when my Dad got hurt one day, I knew I was going to be a nurse," she recalls. "My mother suddenly fainted, so I had to get both of them to a hospital...and that's how my nursing career really started."

Born and raised in Detroit, Carmen eventually found her way to the Toledo Hospital School of Nursing. After graduation she went to work at the University of Michigan Hospital in Ann Arbor. There would be other destinations to follow: a stint at Henry Ford, then on to Holy Cross Hospital and finally Carmen found her home at Beaumont.

Along the way, she married and started the business of raising two sons, and then one day she received the dreaded news: She had cancer. Not your everyday cancer, mind you, a rare cancer with a name most of us couldn't pronounce if it was spelled out on a sheet of paper. Unlike most of us, Carmen the nurse knew exactly what she was in for.

"My prognosis was not good at all," she remembers softly. "But once you're forced to come face to face with your own mortality, somehow it seems to make every day a little more special."

She knew the routine all too well. She endured the heavy doses of chemo. She endured the hair loss and the relentless fatigue, and she believed that one day she would return to the halls of Troy Beaumont cancer-free. She did.

Carmen went back to her patients that were facing the same uncertainties, the same fears, the same questions she had just faced. She was, after all, one of them. Sadly, her grace period only lasted five years before cancer would come to call again and she would be a patient once more.

"The first time you face it you're courageous. You think to yourself, I can win this...I can do this. When it comes back, it's so much harder to convince yourself to fight." The eyes of the patient-nurse begin to glisten at the edges. "Honestly, I didn't think I'd make it."

This time the days passed more slowly. Part of her lung was gone, and the days of chemotherapy seemed to be endless. She had been there and done that before; still, she prepared and longed for the hour that she would be able to return to her post in 5-North. She would be a two-time cancer survivor. But that was not to be.

Almost incredibly, cancer struck again. She had fought

the battle twice; wasn't that enough? This time, the nurse who once claimed to have overdosed on pure happiness was losing her trademark smile.

"I was devastated, depressed," she painfully remembers. "Why not just quit, I must have asked myself a thousand times…but my husband just wouldn't let me."

Carmen's third war with cancer ended over a decade ago. The trademark smile has returned and almost never leaves her countenance these days. It is the same smile she wears every day as she talks and comforts the patients who are her fellow travelers on the fearsome journey she has now completed three times. She knows it as the road to survival, and her own personal experience has become a beacon at the end of that dark pathway for others just like her to follow.

"When you've faced what I've faced, you realize that every day is a gift to you…every day is to be treasured and lived to the fullest."

It's almost sophomoric to say Carmen doesn't take life for granted these days, but we know too many of us do and maybe that's the point of all of this.

As a three-time cancer survivor, she has lived every day to watch her sons grow up. She has lived every day to treasure the face of her first grandchild. She has lived every day to cheer on her beloved Detroit Red Wings to win the Stanley Cup. She has lived every day to celebrate more than thirty years of marriage to her husband, Dennis. She has lived every day to be with the countless patients of Troy Beaumont, to share her wounds and scars with those who must surely believe that she really is the angel of 5-North…on loan to them from God.

The Corridor of Cass

If you happen to be a native Detroiter, you probably already know it by name. If you are a visitor, a cab driver can quickly explain it you. The Cass Corridor, as it's called, is a crazy-quilt of inner city real estate, born in the halcyon days of the auto barons, and all but dismembered in the blight and decay which has dogged the city's recent years of painful transition.

For as long as most can remember, the Corridor has been home to those whom our society would most like to forget. It's the grim sanctuary of the pushers, the prostitutes, the pimps, and mostly the poor; the dark harbor for the cultural flotsam and jetsam of urban neglect.

A little more than two decades ago, when it appeared all but certain the Corridor had been completely disemboweled, the winds of renewal began to stir once again along the street. Houses and buildings here and there were being repaired, renovated, or completely restored. Subtle, almost clandestine forces were joining, not together, but individually to make a statement. "The Corridor will not die this week, nor this month, nor this year because we are here…and you are not." One of those voices belongs to Allen Schaerges.

"You can see it; it's out there in the street. There's a spirit here that's saying something every day." The man sits in a small office in a building that was once a home. It's warm, so an electric fan has to suffice for air conditioning in the room. On the door is pinned a small cartoon depicting the Pope seated next to a likeness of President George W. Bush. The Pope is leaning over to an aide and whispering, "He really is an idiot." While politicians may ignore the Corridor, the Corridor does not ignore the politicians.

Allen Schaerges, pronounced Shar-Jess, is a transplanted suburbanite. He's not a do-gooder from the 'burbs, but a grown-up kid from Berkeley who went to Wayne State's law school, grew old in an ugly war in Vietnam, and came home to live in the Corridor. Now he practices law on the street and preaches the Corridor's salvation.

"When I first came back, I had a small apartment, but I don't know, I guess the place infected me, so I got into a house and started repairing things and well, I'm still repairing things." That's the way it is for those who choose to stake a claim in the forgotten streets that line Cass Avenue. Old doesn't become new overnight.

His years on the streets have earned Allen the unofficial nickname, "the Mayor of the Cass Corridor." It's a moniker well placed. He seems to know most of the area's residents on a first-name basis, along with their personal histories. No real surprise; he has represented his share of them in their moments of distress with the system that works to exclude them.

As well as he knows the people, he knows the old buildings which surround him as he walks to his office each day. He knows their histories, their current state of decline, and the prospects for their future. Allen Schaerges wants no buildings to die on his watch.

There is no progress stampede going on in the Corridor, just little signs of hope that seem to flourish around a lot of disparate corners.

"When you look at the history here, you have to wonder how we let this go. I have to believe that for every building here, there's an opportunity being missed."

Allen points out a sad-looking Victorian house in the lower end of the Corridor. A few children's toys, a Big Wheel tricycle, a shovel and plastic pail rest unattended by a crude sandbox in the corner of the yard. A new cyclone fence runs around the perimeter to keep the children from wandering into the sporadic motor traffic.

"A young couple from the suburbs just moved in here," Allen explains. "They're trying to make it. It's going to be a lot of work, but they want to bring this place back, make it a home. They're committed to the city." It's the same kind of hope Allen brought with him to the Corridor years ago.

Although unknown to most around the city, for over a quarter of a century the Corridor has come alive in an alleyway between Second and Third on the first Saturday after Labor Day. They call it the "Dally in the Alley." It's part art fair, part music festival, and all block party. The Dally has become a cultural *must* for twenty to thirty thousand people every year. It is a communion for the avant-garde held in the long shadows of the Corridor's past. It is a day very, very, close to Allen's heart.

"It's always been something special," Allen observes

with a coy wrinkle around the mouth. "For most people, it's craziness. You've got street vendors, musicians, you name it, all together in the alley doing their thing in separate little places. It's just taken on a life of its own." The sweet smells of barbecue fill the air, as two or three separate strains of music collide in between the shouted conversations of the daily goers. The crowd, if more properly attired, could pass for a group picture at the United Nations. The Dally is the new heartbeat of Cass Avenue.

There are no corporate sponsors for the annual event. They don't want any. The money raised each year from the sale of food, tee-shirts, and beer is plowed right back into the Corridor's streets. The dollars keep the Corridor's heart beating thanks to the handful of hardy souls who delight in calling themselves urban pioneers.

"For those of us here, there is a special feeling, no doubt," the "mayor" says proudly. "I'm not going to tell anybody they can live here without a care, without a problem. My home has been broken into, so you adjust. Maybe you don't own the big-screen TV or the big stereo system. Maybe you're content to read a book. But it's not as bad as people seem to think." The words are honest and earnest. He knows the Corridor is not for everybody.

Understand, there is no great land rush going on south of West Grand Boulevard. There are no deep-pocketed speculators cruising by in Cadillacs to drive up prices, to buy up the old—and put up the new. There is just a spirit in the street, that's all. It's a spirit in the new business that thinks it can make it. It's a spirit to be found in the hope that lingers in the hearts of the people who welcome each new day along the Avenue of Cass.

Golden Years

A Night at the Opera

Only a handful of people knew it was there, silently peering over a busy street corner in the downtown block of Howell, Michigan. It had closed its doors a lifetime ago, but now the brick-lined stairwell is open once again and hopes, as steep as its creaky stairs, are rising that the once-glorious Howell Opera House will find its voice in the community again.

For the past seventy-five of its 125-year history, the opera house has been little more than a mammoth storage closet for the hardware store located at the bottom of its wooden staircase. Now, however, thanks to some very stubborn dreamers, along with a host of local donors and business folks, the Howell Opera House appears poised to play out a new future forged in its own aged footlights.

"See, look at this," commands Jeffrey Stamm, as he taps a finger on a yellowed playbill that was glued to a backstage wall long before either of us was born. "This is the kind of stuff that tells me we have an obligation to save the building and save this heritage from the past."

Jeffrey is one of the stubborn dreamers. As president of the Livingston County Arts Council, he has been the tenor voice of the old opera house. He is a boyish-looking, barrel-chested big man who has become the champion of the drive to save the building, raising his voice among the doubters on a daily basis. You might say Jeffrey is the old theatre's knight in shining armor at the roundtable of the moneychangers.

"Those of us who have a vision," Jeffrey says, "can see past the problems. This is a jewel that needs polishing, but you have to be able to see what's really here to appreciate the history and the potential in its future."

As one might guess, show business does course through Jeffrey's veins. Back in 1979, he was no stranger to the opera house. He was singing at the Metropolitan Opera in New York. At one point, he even performed as the understudy to the great Luciano Pavarotti. The caprices of life and years on the road, however, eventually brought him back to Michigan and to Howell, where he was to assume his new role as the very visible fan of the opera house.

"As you can see, it's still all original," he explains with almost evangelical zeal. "It's still all here. The gas lamps, the wooden chairs, even the shrouds around the footlights in the floor. Of course it needs work, a lot of work, but it's all here and just waiting for us."

It goes without saying that times have changed since 1880 when it took just eleven thousand dollars to build the opera house. Now the pricetag for a sweeping restoration ranges in the millions. That's a lot of money in anybody's checkbook, but no one is lining up to say it can't be done.

Seventy years of silence haven't done the place many favors. The paint has peeled and faded on almost every surface. The windows rattle and don't keep even the slightest draft out. The floorboards creak with more ease than a Halloween haunted house, but one can sense the history nonetheless under the veneer of dust, dirt, and animal droppings. It is that history which the dreamers can clearly see that others, perhaps, cannot.

"We want to bring it back," Jeffrey says. "It's been waiting a very long time for us."

Some of the dusty old stuff will be auctioned off. The discards from the hardware store that have been in storage for years can all go. An antique flit gun that once sprayed DDT on mosquitoes catches the eye. A weathered wooden box with red letters spelling out "Winchester Arms" will lighten some sportsman's wallet. A few of the old theatre's things may have to be sold, but the treasures of Howell's theatrical past will stay to be polished up, painted, or just preserved as is for another age to enjoy and remember.

Just when the footlights will glow again, or when an anxious crowd will fill the lobby with laughter and anticipation, no one can say with any certainty. But the dreamers now own the Opera House and the hardware store downstairs, and that's a good first step toward the goal.

"The Howell community badly needs an arts experience," Jeffrey again pleads. "There are so few of these old buildings left. This could be the cultural center of our community. I'd like to see schoolchildren coming here to put on a pageant or to listen to a symphony orchestra for the first time." Jeffrey Stamm will not surrender this dream.

There are elaborate plans for the future. On the street level, an art gallery and gift shop are supposed to replace the hardware store that's seeking a new location to lease on the west side of town. There are plans to restore virtually everything inside the brick walls and pillared balcony. There are plans for new voices and new sounds to ring forth from the ancient stage where William Jennings Bryan once exhorted his followers. There are plans for new seating where the original Henry Ford once enjoyed the variety of a vaudeville show.

It's just a great dream about a town's history and how to preserve little piece of it for the future.

"I'd like to see this old place just reach out to everyone," Jeffrey concludes. "After all, there is more to life than TV."

Amen, Jeffrey, Amen!

The More Things Change...

It managed to survive for 125 years and eight months. During its long and prolific life, it chronicled the good times and the bad times of a little Michigan town in the course of three very different centuries.

It was a true community newspaper, full of local stuff about local folks doing local things. Perhaps, if it had been one of those big-time, big-city daily papers, more mention of its untimely passing might have been made, but in once-rural Richmond, Michigan, the *Richmond Review* died peacefully on a cold February morning. In its passing, the *Review* left behind a simple legacy of neighborly honesty, volumes of yellowed pages from its humble past, and more than a few heart-wrenched mourners.

"It's just a bottom-line decision," says Alice Brandel, the proud about-to-be ex-editor of the weekly newspaper. "I have to choke back the tears just to talk about it," she says, failing to choke back the tears.

The *Richmond Review* began its mission way back in June of 1876. It printed then, as it has until now, the kind of news that really doesn't change much over the years. The

173

paper reported the births and the deaths in town. It reported the school announcements, the engagements and marriages, and who was doing what around the place. No heavy stuff usually, but in 125 years and eight months, the *Review* did write the history of a little Michigan village, a village that became a city, and a city that has nearly become another suburb to Detroit.

"If you look back into these dusty volumes, you can read the little history of the people and the history of the town. From the weddings to the funerals to the closing of the millinery shop on Main Street in 1933." It's true, the huge black binders that hold the dried and corner-tattered pages of the past speak volumes in dark ink on nearly yellow paper.

"When I look back on these pages, I can see there are still so many things that were there back then and are still here with us today," says Brandel.

In the early years of its second century, the rural farmers of Richmond learned about things like the sinking of the *Titanic* and about their men who went off to war. That stuff was usually on the front page. Flip over a page or two, and they were reading about Will Potter's purchase of the Photoplay Theatre in town. On the same page was an item about the closing of the Curry sisters' millinery shop.

In the 1920s, the *Review* was worried about keeping the kids down on the farm. In its final editions, the *Review* has been worrying about just keeping the farms. The times in little Richmond have drastically changed, and the paper has reflected those changes, for better and for worse, in its weekly pages. It has always been there, every Wednesday for over a century. In fact, folks don't even call it Wednesday in Richmond, Memphis, and New Haven. They call it *Review* day.

"I sure hope somebody still cares about babies being born, and people getting married, and kids who make the honor roll in their school." The words seem to bring that choke back again to the young newspaperwoman who seems so moved by the things that didn't even happen in her own past.

For a good many months there were hopes that someone, or something, might suddenly step in to save the *Review's* fading life, but at the final hour there was no reprieve and no pardon. The printing press had finally run out of time, ink, paper, and most importantly, money.

"It's hard to accept...hard to believe. I guess I don't want to accept what's happening. A community newspaper is so important," pleads the young woman who is losing a job and an aged friend. "A community newspaper binds a community together; it pretty much creates a community, in fact." It's a good argument to hold on to, but it no longer carries any weight where it matters.

When established traditions come to an abrupt end, the real issues behind the demise are usually complex and financially driven. These are difficult times in the newspaper trade, what with all the competition from radio, TV, and nowadays, the Internet. Then again, maybe we've just outgrown our sense of community. Maybe we, as a society, have outgrown our previous need for neighborly news. Doesn't make much sense when you think about it, but things are never going to be quite the same in Richmond.

Review Day is gone, and all those empty white paper chutes that dot the old town's dirt roads and the new city's manicured streets will only serve now, as a haunting reminder, that the more things change...the more things change.

They Call It
"The Blues"

"I've got a cold, cold feelin'…It's jus' like ice around my heart." The words of a well-worn song moaned into a round-topped microphone on a stage bathed in the color of a faded spotlight. Glasses clink in the background; conversations are muted by the music that spills out of some tattered speakers affixed to an adjacent wall. Smoke curls in the air. That's why they call it the blues.

It is uniquely American music, born in the cotton fields of slavery, raised as an anguished anthem of the sprawling city. It is raw, relentless, a timeless energy, released in the bend of a steel string that cries of lost love, heartbreak, disappointment, turmoil, passing pleasures and pain. It's the stuff of life distilled in smoke, whiskey, and the bond of common suffering.

"The blues is pretty tough stuff," says a man who should know. Bruce Iglauer has been a friend and fan of the music since he can't remember when. His love of the blues has all but consumed his life. "The blues is tough, and when you water it down, it stops being blues. That hardness of emotion, that directness of emotions is what makes it the blues."

177

The music's humble structure is, quite simply, an elixir to stir the human soul. Its plaintive phrasing and pungent lyrics have never gained widespread popularity, yet the music is considered to be the root of every music form from jazz to rock to country.

"Hey man, rock 'n roll is the blues, all of it," says saxophone veteran A.C. Reed. The longtime Chicago musician has made his living with his horn for six decades, so he should know. "I was playin' that stuff before rock 'n roll came in. Man, I've played all kinds of music, but you know, it all done come from the blues."

For the most part, the music remains unchanged. The same basic chords are always there, but with variations as different as the skin tones of those who play them. Each offers an interpretation of the fundamental human truths first defined in the plantation fields and then later in the ghettoes of America's African-American culture.

The Windy City has always enjoyed the reputation of being the blues capital of the United States. The people in Chicago care for the music, and they go out of their way to make sure visitors and residents alike hear the blues in "Chi-town."

Of course, the blues knows no geographic boundaries, no economic boundaries. Its only perimeter is the ear of the listener, and to get an earful these days, one almost always has to drop into a dimly lit lounge in a not-so-nice part of town, because that's where the blues is at.

"There's a media problem, an image problem with the blues," says Bruce Iglauer. He took his passion for the music and put it on vinyl years ago, making his first record in what would become an independent label success known as Alligator Records. Today, he brings the blues to the world on compact discs, but it is a small audience that awaits each new release.

"People think it's sad music, that it's old people's music," Iglauer laments. "They think it's music played by a bunch of irresponsible drunks, that it's technically unsophisticated. They seem to think anybody can play the blues. It's this kind of an image problem that's the big enemy."

As Bruce waxes philosophically about the music, the clock reads 4:00 A.M. and the blues rolls on from the bandstand.

Say hello to Albert Collins. His home is a 1950s vintage GMC bus. His address is the highway, somewhere between Boston and Bakersfield. If you want his phone number, you'll have to listen for it somewhere in the strings of his battered Fender Telecaster guitar.

"I'll never be a rich man," Albert says with the reluctance of acceptance, and the honesty of achievement. "When I play it makes people smile, and makes me feel good." This humble Texan from a dirt town called Leona is destined for bigger things in his world of blues, but he doesn't know it as he sits quietly on a sofa, a white and black husky dog curled on the floor next to his comfortable ostrich-skin cowboy boots.

Outside, on a loading dock that serves as a patio for his band members, the beer flows as freely as the conversations. The night air is punctuated by laughter. The between-sets recorded music filters out of the open doorway and spills across the asphalt parking lot. It is another night on the road for the Icebreakers, Albert's always-changing band of brothers.

There is very little romance in the gritty life of the blues. Rather, it is a grueling procession of sameness. Life on the road is a progression of performances, punctuated by fleeting highs that are all too quickly dissolved by the monotony of drunken compliments and broken promises.

From the stage, Albert once again moans the familiar lyrics of the blues. "They cut my lights off this mornin'… threw my furniture out the door…I heard on the news this mornin'…it's gonna come rain or snow…I've got the pneumonia…" Between each verse, the strangely tuned Telecaster whines in a brittle accompaniment, filling the voiceless voids with an echo of the painful words just spoken. It's the blues, up close and personal, and for real.

It is, by any standard, life on the ragged edge. Day is night, and night is right, and the good times are measured in the redundant revolutions of the rolling wheel. It is living on the highway where time is calculated not by the clock, but by the succession of endless road signs, budget motels, and the bars of the music.

When the coach stops, there is time to kill. If he's in the mood, Albert loves a good hand of blackjack, a game at which he excels. It usually leads to the recovery of some of the money he has doled out to the band boys after the last gig. Albert drives the old bus, and when the bus stops, so does everything else. It often stops where the Colonel serves chicken. This time, it has stopped in Palo Alto, California for a game of dominoes in his mother-in-law's garage.

As the band boys listen to some tapes on a boom box, the hours pass and grow late. Tonight they are scheduled to play on the Sunset Strip in L.A. It's a long way from Palo Alto.

"Isn't it time to hit the highway?" someone asks as the dominoes fall for another game.

Albert, undisturbed by the clock, agrees and ambles to the bus. "I'm gonna fire up, right now," he says. Somebody calculates the progression of the trip to Los Angeles at four miles an hour. "Maybe we'll have to stop in Santa Barbara and catch a plane." Albert replies with the laugh that is his trademark among friends. The diesel fires, and they're on the road again.

Albert is fond of saying that if trouble was money, he'd be a millionaire. Thirty years on the road have left him a very rich man by those standards. Yes, he did have a gold record back in the early 1960s, and his recent albums have often been Grammy nominees, but crossover success has been elusive. He can, however, count his friends in the hundreds and his admirers in the thousands.

One of them is George Thorogood. "Whew, Albert's style is—well, he's more of a guitarist extraordinaire," the pop-blues icon explains. He has come to see the show at the Lingerie Lounge on the Strip. "Albert's an extraordinary musician and showman, whereas I'm more of a thief and a bullshitter," he laughs as fans in the crowd suddenly come over to the table to say hello or shake his hand.

The night wears on in Los Angeles and concludes with a stinging rendition of Albert's big hit, "Frosty," an up-tempo shuffle in the Texas tradition that has become his signature set ender. It goes on forever, as the showman dazzles the faithful at the end of his one-hundred-foot cord. He has walked every square inch of the bar, and concludes the evening with a stroll up and down the sidewalk, waving to the passing cars that fade into the neon glow along the Sunset Strip. As his followers watch in amazement, Albert Collins once again becomes the pied piper of the blues.

It used to be that if you were looking for a suitcase full of the blues in Detroit, you had to pick up that baggage at the Soup Kitchen Saloon. The Motor City was a major blues town in the days when Hasting Street was alive and well. Sadly, that era is gone, and now Detroit is just another stop on the circuit for the modern minstrels of the blues.

Not too long ago, a young Detroiter named Robert Noll was busy teaching guitar lessons in a suburban music shop. In the 1980s, he was one of the new breed of blues players like Stevie Ray Vaughn, who were re-energizing the old, and bringing fresh new interpretations to the new blues.

"I love the blues thing because that's what I feel," says the young man with the vintage Gibson guitar resting on his right thigh. "I like the people, I like working with these guys, and there's a lot to be said about the art part of it." Rob's licks on the old guitar caught the eye of Albert Collins on a visit to Detroit in 1982. To his surprise, the man he has learned to call "Pops" invited him to join his band.

"Sometimes it gets really rough out here on the road," says Rob. "But when you get there, and you know you're gonna get up there on that stage…well then, you know everything's gonna be all right for three or four hours. But then you get back on the bus and you know you've got so many miles ahead…and you know, man, it's just a hard life." They are words from a relative rookie in the true life of a bluesman.

"Blues people are in a world all by themselves," says another veteran of the music, Brian McDonald, who has been an impresario of the blues in Detroit since 1976. When others had turned their backs on the limited audience appeal of the music, Brian opened the doors to the now-famous Soup Kitchen Saloon. He knows the music and those who love to make it.

"I find that blues people are used to being on the down side of things. It's sad to say, but they are people who are used to having to sweat it out. Many times they are treated unfairly or they're greatly underpaid for their talents. They have a lot of legitimate reasons to have the blues." Brian speaks directly from his heart. "It may sound trite, but it's true. Most blues players are truly professional and they have gone years without receiving the proper recognition or the financial success that should go with it," he says.

Backstage once again, in a tiny dressing room with greenish walls scarred by plaster pock marks and hastily scribbled signatures of the players who have come before him, Albert Collins sits alone, tuning his legendary Fender guitar. In his mouth rests a harmonica, used as a makeshift tuning device to bring the stainless strings of his guitar into their proper misalignment. As his feet tap in rhythm of the music that filters into the room, a glass of Jack Daniels sits and giggles its liquid contents to the beat. The ostrich boots are always there to hold up through another show, another walk along the bar, another stroll into the street where there will be more fans in line awaiting a second show.

Albert Collins has come to town again. The pied piper is back to lead the faithful on another musical tour in another bar in another town. Historically, the blues has always come to the party dressed in black. But in the changing times, and in the changing music of an ending century, one doesn't have to be black to have, live, or love the blues.

Another show over, from the doorway of the battered blue bus, the music flows acappella into the night air. "The highway is like a woman...soft shoulders and dangerous curves..."

Note: Albert Collins was my dearest friend. At the age of sixty-one, he succumbed to cancer in November 1993 at the peak of his career. He died having achieved at least a measure of the recognition he so rightfully deserved. I miss him today, and include this story in tribute to his memory. He left us a very rich man because he made us smile.

Some Horses Do Go to Heaven

Inside a weathered cedar fence, they stand quietly peering out at the world. These are not the proud, regal, perfect animals of the Kentucky breeders. If they could talk, however, they'd quickly tell us they haven't died yet, but they have gone to heaven in South Lyon, Michigan.

They are the tired, the abused, the wretched, the aged, the neglected, even the abandoned, but inside these spacious corrals they are safe in a place called Horses' Haven.

"Oooh, you're my baby aren't you?" Gently she soothes the grayish mare with a pat. It's clear from the first glance that there is a long-established trust between animal and caretaker.

Barb Baker had the dream a few years back to provide a special place, a haven for horses, which have always been so close to her heart. It wasn't easy, but with the help of a few other compassionate and caring horse lovers, Horses' Haven became a reality.

"This is Ruthie." Barb's introduction seems directed more to the ancient animal than to her visitor. "She's about twenty-five years old. Now the reason she wears the bell is because 'Buddy' over there is blind and we don't want him to feel lonesome. He can hear the bell and know just where Ruthie is." Across the corral stands another senior citizen of this strange equestrian place so devoid of the pomp and circumstance one usually associates with the horsey set.

At any given time, there may be twenty or thirty horses at the Haven. It's way too much for Barb to handle alone, so thanks to a dedicated posse of volunteers, the stalls get cleaned, the horses fed, the medications dispensed, and the fences mended.

Barb is never short with her praise for their efforts. "Well, the volunteers come in each day about 7:00 A.M. and they first have to do all the feeding." As she walks slowly through the stalls in the big barn she continues her recitation of the routine. "All of the horses here are on their own special diets, whatever it takes to keep them up." With her sense of humor showing, she says it's really a gourmet restaurant for horses.

"We have a clipboard chart for each one so everybody knows what they eat, what their special medications are, if they need any medical work done. Then they just come outside and spend the rest of the day in the fields."

It's all very simple. It's good-hearted people keeping perfectly sound animals alive for another day, or another month, or another year. There's no glue factory or foreign dinner plate in the future for the horses of this haven.

Where, one asks, do these horses come from? Barb's answer is short and direct. "They come from all over. They're throwaways." People don't throw away horses, do they? "Just like you throw the garbage out, or throw away a broken cof-

fee cup. That's what most of these horses are…throwaways."
It's difficult truth to accept.

While the horses are definitely close to Barb's emotional heart, there is something very special about her physical heart as well. It's new. Okay, maybe it's more precise to call it previously owned. Two years ago, Barb underwent a heart transplant operation, so it's still new to her. It's a big heart too, with plenty of additional room for even more of her four-legged friends.

"How do I keep up?" she answers the question with a question. "These horses keep me going. I have to try and keep up with them. I know the Haven needs not only me, but it needs every one of the volunteers who come here every day…and it needs someone with vision to see the plans through and down the road a number of years from now. We have to expand, and we will expand." The answer has become Barb's anthem of health and reason for being. Once again, her humor and dedication come through in her concluding thought. "I don't know how we're gonna do it all, but we are gonna do it…we're gonna do it somehow."

There are still many dreams for this heaven for horses. In the meantime, the business of caring for uncared-for horses continues each day without much fanfare. It's just a lot of hard work, love, and compassion for the castoffs and the throwaways with the big brown eyes that almost seem to reflect gratitude and appreciation when the special lady with the new heart, as big as a horse, walks by.

"It's been a very rewarding life for me," she says as her feet take her past the empty stalls and into the short field behind the red barn. "I guess I can't ask for more than that…"

Pete the Barber

In the blow-dried age of styling gel, mousse, and extra-firm holding spray, in the world of upscale beauty shops, salons, and franchised mall stores for hair, Pete the barber is outstanding in his field.

"Dollar-fifty, that's what I charged," Pete says, explaining the good old days when he first started trimming unruly manes in Detroit. "I charged a dollar-fifty and I used to make good money—maybe two hundred dollars a week."

The truth is, Pete's been outstanding in his field for well over forty years now. Comb and scissors in hand, he's there six days a week in the little shop right under the People Mover in Greektown. Nothing fancy about it; one might not even know it was there, except for the sign that is painted over the storefront door.

Many heads have rolled into Pete's place and all of them have left looking and feeling much better. It's a good haircut, but it's Pete that makes everybody feel good.

"Lotta people come and go...Lotta people come to Pete's barber shop...lotta lawyers, lotta policeman. I enjoy

189

over here," Pete says in a thick Greek accent. The words are precisely what one would expect from the big man behind the chair. His hair is lightly sprinkled with gray these days, the beltline has acquired an inch or three in the passing of his youth, and the light blue barber smock he wears seems to brighten the intensity of his dark eyes.

"If you make up your mind, you wanna be some-thin'...this country make you a success...you gotta lotta opportunities here." This is the serious side of Pete Kithas, and he means every word of it.

For all these years, Pete's bread and butter has come right off the top of many of Detroit's finest. Pete does cops: commanders, lieutenants, sergeants, detectives, and patrol-men on the beat. If they have hair on their heads, it's likely to come off at Pete's. He's been in his shop so long, he's even doing the heads of cops who have long since retired.

In the single chair in the middle of the shop sits Jim, a cop. Maturity has removed much of what used to sit on the top of Jim's head, but he wouldn't trust the sides to anyone else but Pete. Jim happens to be one of the retirees that keep coming back to the little shop under the People Mover.

Pete is very proud of his repeat business. "Thirty two years I been cuttin' his hair. He's retired now, but he still comes back here 'cause he finds nobody cuts his hair like me." This barber is never without a smile.

Things haven't changed a lot at Pete's place over the years. That's part of the charm, part of the story. In a cor-ner of the small shop, an ancient space heater glows with blue and yellow flames. It looks old enough to have been condemned by one of those federal safety agencies, but it does work really well.

It's not encouraged, but smoking is definitely allowed. A glance around the place makes that obvious from the circular ashtrays that sport not only ashes, but several butts including one well-burned cigar. On a chrome-legged table, one can also find a wide selection of magazines that appeal to gentlemen of distinction, and others who just like to look at naked women. An occasional cuss word is okay by Pete.

You could probably say Pete's modest establishment is a holdout in a world where it seems to have become a little more confusing to be a man these days.

One of Pete's regular customers has his picture prominently displayed behind the second barber chair. It is a man in a United States Marine uniform, Major Greg Raths. A veteran of the conflict in the Gulf in the early 1990s, Major Raths dropped a bomb on Iraq with Pete's name painted on it during that brief war. Well, as things turn out, Major Raths, now a colonel, came home and ended up being assigned to the White House. Suddenly, guess who gets invited for a personal tour of 1600 Pennsylvania Avenue?

"Before I know, we walkin' around...I see the President coming with his security...I walk up, I say, 'How you doin' Mr. President? I'm Pete the barber from Michigan...I vote for you alla time. I vote for you two times.'" The story is punctuated with chuckles and a sense of self-amazement at his own bravado.

William Jefferson Clinton was obviously charmed by the encounter, ordered a picture of the occasion, autographed it later, and now it hangs in a place of serious honor in Pete's barber shop. Not even a President of the United States, it seems, can escape the gregarious Greek ambassador of the Motor City.

Incidentally, Pete's no stranger to the military himself. As a dashing young man with a pencil-thin moustache, he served in the Greek Army's equivalent of the Green Berets. A photo of the time also hangs on the wall behind his always-busy red leather chair. He remembers his days in the special forces with pride. The photograph is fading in the sunlight that pours through the plate glass window, but it was taken long before he adopted America back in 1956.

That's probably the long and the short of it at Pete's Barber Shop. The long hair is on the floor; the short hair is out the door. If your travels happen to take you downtown, honk if you're driving by, or wave if you're riding the People Mover to the casino. If he's not talking with a customer, Pete will smile and wave back to you, just to make you feel good.

"So, Smitty, how you wanna cut it—short on the sides today with a little off atop? Okay now, did I tella you about the time..."

Requiem for an Old Tiger

She still looks good for her age. At eighty-six, she still has a sparkle in her sunlit eyes. She still has magic in her heart. She still has history in her soul. But her once-hardy frame has grown tired. It is weak in places now, and while she is still able to smile back at us, we all know it's now just a matter of time.

There was time enough for another visit. There was time enough to recall when we were both much younger. There was time enough to say a proper goodbye.

For almost a century, she lived at the same address. She did change her name a few times. Yes, she did have some cosmetic attention over the years. But for those who knew her best, there was always the comforting assurance that she was something special, something very special, and so to know her was to love her.

"I don't know, it's just something I can't really explain," says a senior citizen, sporting an ever-present navy blue hat. "I just get a thrill every time I walk in here. I've probably spent more time in here than I have at home," he concludes in a half chuckle.

If Tiger Stadium could speak, one has the feeling it would be with his voice. After all, Ernie Harwell is no stranger in her midst, so maybe she really does speak in Ernie's voice, because through him she has come alive on so many nights and sun-drenched days when her words, through his voice, took us to her side and to the boys of each summer who came to play a child's game on her emerald lawn.

"There have been so many great moments here," Ernie recalls as his feet leave brief footprints in the grass that is trimmed so perfectly around the monumental flag pole. "There were so many great names who played on this field. I remember Ted Williams, and Mickey Mantle, Joe DiMaggio, Charley Maxwell, Norm Cash, and Gibbie." He could go on endlessly reciting the names in her golden past. They had all come to call on the lady at one time, and most of them took a memory back home with them.

She sent her sons to war, and she was there to welcome them back home. She had a knack for filling her house with heroes, some for a day, some of them forever.

She endured the wars, an ugly depression, several recessions, a strike or two, two urban riots, and the plague of blight that swept through her neighbors' streets. Through all of it, she held fast: A beacon that called us back every year when the winter's wind gave way to the crocus and the daffodil and a man in a black suit would yell, "Play ball."

She adopted many children in her time. There was a strange curmudgeon named Cobb, a catcher named Bennett, a skinny kid named Kaline. Those names come to the mind quickly, but there were so many more.

There was a kid named Erik who came to her door more than a half-century ago, and never forgot his first meeting.

And, of course, there was the gentle man who now speaks her words, who has come to tell us that her time has come. It's time, he says, to let her go.

"Yeah, it's time," he says with the kind of acceptance that only maturity and peace in one's own soul affords. "She had her day. She's just gotten too old. The demands of the game have changed now. You have to have the suites and all the amenities fans expect these days. I guess it's a little hard to say goodbye, but it's definitely time."

Goodbyes for most of us don't come easily, but the time for the final goodbye has come. The seasons will change again, as Ernie so ably reminds us each spring from his honored place in the booth above home plate. The boys of summer will be gone at the final out on the final day, and the lights will go out. The traffic at Michigan and Trumbull will thin out, the parking lots will empty, the toasts will be heard in the Dugout bar, and that will be the end of it.

In time, a new park will open in another part of town and there will be much to celebrate. In time, there will be new traditions and new memories, and new names will be added to the pantheon of the past. For now, we accept the passing of a great lady at the corner. May it always be said that she lived out her days with a Tiger's heart.

Muttsy's Mission

More than four million Americans may be there now—a place where the familiar has become the unfamiliar, where the routine has become the difficult, where the recognized has become the unrecognizable. It is the heartwrenching world of Alzheimer's disease.

"I brought you something," the lady in the white turtleneck sweater says, staring into the vacant eyes of an elderly woman sitting cockeyed in a well-used wheelchair. "Isn't he precious?" she asks, hoping for some kind of response. The pause turns into an endless wait.

The woman in the turtleneck is Fran Maiers. She is no stranger to this strange world. She watched helplessly as her mother's life and love slipped away into the living limbo that so mystifies and terrifies us. For a time before her death, Fran's mother called her "Amy"—not her name, just a name which spontaneously emerged from the fog of her dimming mind. Now, to Fran, the name "Amy" has taken on a special meaning. It is the name of a crusade to, as Fran says, "remember those who no longer can." She calls it "Amy's Muttsy Mission."

The sole purpose of the Muttsy Mission is to place a soft, furry, loveable little stuffed dog named Muttsy into the hands and hearts of those who are trapped in the confounding grasp of Alzheimer's disease.

It all began with a visit to a nursing home, as Fran explains. "I came to the nursing home at Christmastime to sing some carols to the patients. As I was packing up to leave, I saw a lady sitting in a wheelchair off to the side, and she had this little stuffed dog on her lap." It was to be the beginning of Amy's Muttsy Mission. "She just kept petting, stroking the dog...so I went over and put my arms around her and asked her about her dog. That image is still riveted in my mind. When I left, I just said to myself, somehow, some way, I'm going to give one of those dogs to my mother and to all of my mom's friends."

No team of psychiatrists, no gerontologists, no social workers accompany Amy's mission. It's usually just Fran Myers and some other caring volunteers and Muttsy, on a journey of compassion. Front and center on each visit is the little dog which seems able to bring a smile to a face that's misplaced the reflex, or perhaps return a sparkle to an eye dulled by too many hours of incomprehension. It's just Muttsy and a hug from "Amy" and some gently whispered words. The mission is accomplished for a moment, even if the moment passes too quickly.

Fran leans in toward the elderly woman who sits vacantly in her wheelchair. The mouth is open, the chin drooping, but not dropped. "Marlene, dear, I brought you something," Fran quietly says close to the woman's ear.

Marlene nods to the sound, looks down at the dog and asks quickly, "Does he bark?" No, he doesn't bark, she's assured, and the woman's hand begins to stroke the back of the stuffed animal.

No one, it seems, can explain what happens between the little plush toy and its new owner. There's nothing in the medical literature of our time to detail the interaction or its consequences. Something happens, that's all, and something is good.

"No, we don't know how it works," Fran is quick to add. "I'm asked about that a lot. It's just between Muttsy and God and the Alzheimer's patient. It just works, that's all...and it's amazing. One lady held the dog and she looked up at me and said, 'Now I have a family again.'" That is the magic of Muttsy.

People across the country have seen it happen too. Now Fran, the daughter who was temporarily named Amy, is trying to put a Muttsy on the lap of every Alzheimer's sufferer she can meet, free of charge.

"We send them through the mail," she says. "They fit perfectly in a Priority Mail envelope, and for three dollars and sixty cents apiece we have probably sent three hundred of them around the United States."

The little stuffed dogs named Muttsy are manufactured by the Gund Company. They're not cheap (each one costs about fifteen dollars), so donations are always needed to help fulfill the promise of Amy's mission.

In just a little over six years, more than a thousand Muttsys have found new homes on new laps in new places. Hopes are high that the mission can do even more in the years ahead. It has been a rewarding but nonetheless difficult journey.

What began in a nursing home has come full circle for Fran Maiers. On this day, she has brought the original Muttsy back to its original owner. She has come to the place where she first saw the floppy little dog with the synthetic coat. The fur on Muttsy's back has been stroked almost flat by the incessantly wandering hands of its first owner. It was here, in a bed by a window, in a room with yellow paint and little more, that Amy's Muttsy Mission began.

It is an ongoing mission, one which may never be completed until the darkened pathway to a cure for Alzheimer's disease is finally illuminated.

"He says bye-bye," the frail voice speaks from the bed.

"Yes, Marlene, yes, he's saying bye-bye," Fran softly responds, as the weakened hands return once again to the comfort of Muttsy's synthetic fur.

Don on the Farm

It is an early morning in March, when spring is justifiably anticipated, but the sawteeth in the air tell the nose and earlobes that spring's legitimate arrival usually has nothing to do with the calendar in Michigan. It doesn't matter, however. If it were the coldest day of the year, Don Staebler would still be outside tending his flock, just as he has done every day for more days than most of us will ever live.

It is the worst cliché to write that life on the farm is a lot of hard work, but how else can one express it? It's the truth, and Don Staebler knows it better than anyone. After all, he's lived it, and loved it every day of his very long life.

"I've been here nearly ninety years," he says quietly but firmly. "Been here all the time, except during the War." He speaks of the time when Franklin Roosevelt was President. Of the time when young men were called to serve their country for a purpose well understood, and accomplished with determination.

When your lifetime has generously stretched across nine decades, virtually all of it spent on the same body of land, when you have watched your father work the fields, and your mother preserve the bounty of the harvest before another winter calls, then it's not just eighty-seven acres of trees and fertile soil, it's eighty-seven acres of your heart. That's why Don Staebler couldn't just let it go.

He couldn't let the brokers, the speculators, and the moneychangers buy their way into his heartland. The land, with the ponds where he bathed as a child, just couldn't, shouldn't, and wouldn't become another field of someone else's dreams.

"I wanted to keep it whole. They came at me with all kinds of ideas. They wanted a chunk here, or a piece over there, and I just kept on telling them no...no, I'm not going to let you grow houses on my farm." The passion of his words almost seems to restore the sparkle of youth to his eyes. His determination is as solid as the foundation of the old house of hand-hewn timbers.

When Don was a little younger, the 125 paces from the house to the barnyard stepped off a good deal faster. He didn't have to wait back then for the motor traffic to pass on the country dirt road that separated the acres and the house from the barn. Back then, his neighbors were all farmers too. Now, they're lawyers, doctors, or engineers who have built English Tudor replicas on the farmland, and drive their BMWs to Starbucks every Saturday morning. Now the forty-seven head of cattle loitering around his big red barn is the last herd to be found between Ann Arbor and eastward to Detroit's city limits.

"Sometimes I have to wait ten or fifteen minutes for the traffic to clear, just so I can walk across the street to take care of the animals. There are so many people out here now."

His simple sentences underscore the difficulty in accepting the transitions that accompany the inevitabilities of passing time and change.

Nobody has ever said living is easy, except perhaps in a song. Over a decade ago, Don lost the love of his life. His beloved wife Lena passed away, but not before they enjoyed a warm anniversary celebration at their church. It's a day to be remembered, captured in a photograph and carefully placed upon the mantel above the stone fireplace.

Soon after Lena's death, as if the loneliness were not enough to cope with, Don was diagnosed with cancer. It was not easy, but he still managed to feed his livestock every day through the thirty-nine days of intensive but debilitating radiation treatments. Then, one day, along came Mary. She was the widow of Don's older brother, and now as it had so many times before, the land was there to mend not one, but two broken hearts.

"Well, I couldn't let the cancer beat me." Don says as if it were that easy. Mary smiles a knowing smile at the man across the table. It's a regular morning routine. A cup of coffee, maybe two. Time to talk and share a memory. A house cat curls on the braided rug beneath their feet.

While Don Staebler has all but defied the aging process that has claimed the virility of men much younger than he, ninety years have still passed in his life. With no children to take over his daily chores, or to tend the land, the passage of his time has become a threat. The land must stay, but how? It is the question that has been sitting in one of the back corners of his mind for a long time. The land must stay as he tended it. It must stay as he has loved it. It must stay as he will one day leave it.

The answer arrived when Washtenaw County came to call one day. The men in the suits wanted to talk about a new idea for a public park in the area. Don Staebler was listening.

"Oh, they were full of ideas," he says with a half-smile, half-smirk. "They wanted to put a swimming pool over on one side, one of those petting zoos over there past the barn…they had roads running all through the place." Suffice it to say, it was not exactly what Don had envisioned, but he wasn't writing the idea off, either.

It took some time, but the county suits and the country farmer found some middle ground in their talks about the land. Some of the big ideas shrunk a little, the dollars defined themselves a bit better, and a deal was basically done as far as Don Staebler was concerned.

If, as he says, he wanted to grow houses, he no doubt could have turned his heartland into a huge cash crop. Instead, Don took a million or so less to save his dream fields, his pristine ponds, the forty-seven head of cattle in the barn across the road, and the priceless memories of his childhood, his parents, a loving marriage, and an old age lived well and happily.

The farm will become a new public park in Washtenaw County. Don and Mary will live out their days in the old farmhouse rent-free, and hopefully carefree. Perhaps the county will even see fit to name the new place "Staebler Park." Maybe they can erect the sign near the spot where Don Staebler will continue to cross Plymouth Road to tend his flock in all those mornings yet to come.

They really should, you know?

The Boys of Summer

Consider it a breath of fresh air in the world of sports. A world dominated by shoe endorsements, comedy beer commercials and too many athletes with attitude. On this groomed field, we find a bunch of older men playing baseball because they love the competition, but most of all, they just love the game.

"Oh, it's just fun," one of the players says. "It's so nice to be a kid again two or three times a week."

This is the world of senior softball and it's sort of a serious business. You see, there's a world championship tournament coming to Taylor, Michigan again and these guys aim to play in it.

Okay, let's be honest here. They all ache a little more these days. The zip in the old fastball has been zapped. And the eyes may not be quite as eagle-sharp as they were when they tried out for the senior high team a few decades back, but what the heck, it is still the same game and they're out there playing it just like before. Playing every inning in fact, because they love the game.

"You know, I'm seventy-two years old," one player says. "Hey, I've still got a little color and a little hair left. Just being out here brightens your outlook on things. You look forward to it."

His team has just moved up a notch in the rankings. They're in the over-seventy division now, which gives you a pretty good idea about the average age of the squad they've assembled.

Once upon a time, they were cops, lawyers, teachers, plumbers, or salesmen. Now, at least two or three times a week, they are ballplayers again, intent on winning and making certain they have a good time doing it.

"We've been playing against these same teams for years now, same bunch of guys," says one of the gray hairs. "We all know each other by our first names."

The uniforms don't measure up to major league standards of course. If they're lucky, maybe a local hardware store will pick up the tab for tee-shirts and some caps. This year, one of the teams hit the jackpot. They're being sponsored by a major funeral home.

"Well, they look at us as potential customers, I guess," one of the men jokes. "But not for a while, anyway."

The balls, the gloves, and particularly the bats are getting a little expensive for the fixed-income set these days. No matter; it's not about the money or the sponsors. They'll tell you icily that this is not a fashion show. This is about playing ball.

No, winning isn't everything on this field of friendly dreams. Winning will never be the only thing either, because this is a game about the game and the enduring friendships it fosters each and every time they take to the basepaths.

"We enjoy playing against each other. It's just such a joy to be out here," a player proclaims. "I think a lot of it is just the competitiveness of it all. I mean, we're really competitive."

It is a full season each year for these ageless man-boys of summer. Certainly they have put a few more summers under their sagging beltlines than those wet-behind-the ears kids who play for all that big money in the big ballparks.

But don't you have to wonder who's really playing from the heart? I think we know the answer.

In a League of Her Own

The game is called America's national pastime. At the beginning of a new century, there are some who argue that the game is past its time, but that is a debate not suited for this story. This is the story of Mary Moore, who has carried with her a passion for the game almost every day of her satisfied life.

She can't tell you when she fell in love with the game called baseball. It doesn't matter, of course, and it doesn't change the way baseball changed her. It's just a fact that some six decades ago, the game that really belonged to men held an unflagging fascination for her. So, when she could, she played her heart out.

Things haven't changed much over the long haul for Mary. She is still thrilled by the crack of the bat, the feel of fresh resin on the fingers, and the special camaraderie that is born in the throes of heated competition on the field. The truth is, when it comes to the ball diamond, Mary Moore is in a league of her own, and in a class all by herself.

209

That's probably why she had a cameo appearance in the Hollywood movie. If you missed seeing *A League of Their Own*, it's a movie about women's baseball. It's about a handful of sports pioneers who made history in the 1940s and early '50s, playing big-league professional baseball.

In some ways, it still seems like yesterday to Mary. "Well, it was a lot of fun," she begins in tones too modest for the sense of pride which shows plainly on her face. "We didn't get paid a lot, but we had a lot of fun. If we were on the touring team, we got about twenty-five dollars a week. If you were lucky enough to be picked up by one of the home teams, you got fifty-five dollars a week." Nobody was getting rich in women's baseball.

They called it the "All-American Girls Baseball League."

Obviously it is a reflection of the less politically-correct times. The league was made up of teams with names like the "Springfield Sallies" and the "Battle Creek Belles." No, they didn't make a lot of money, but as Mary says, they did have a lot of fun. They even had the chance to play in some of the great parks like Yankee Stadium.

"It was something to walk out on that field," Mary recalls. "Casey Stengel was the manager." She begins to recite a list of Yankee names, the Who's Who in baseball at the time. "Oh, there was Joe DiMaggio, Phil Rizzuto, Whitey Ford, and Billy Martin…they were all there. I was pretty nervous."

Mary Moore was making a real name for herself in her first year in the "majors." She was leading the way in hits, total bases, RBIs, and even home runs, when it all suddenly ended. Her career snapped with the sound of a bone in her ankle.

"I had a hit or a walk...I don't remember, but I was on base, running for second. I slid in, and I guess I hooked one of my cleats on the bag as I was sliding around, and I twisted my ankle and heard it snap. Everyone came running and they had to help me off the field. Jimmy Foxx, the Hall of Famer, actually carried me off the field." A baseball legend helping a legend in-the-making to gracefully exit her too-short career.

For Mary, her days in professional baseball had ended at second base that day. The All-American Girls Baseball League didn't last a lot longer. It didn't survive the 1950s. The Great War was over, the boys were back home, the postwar period produced boom times, and "girls" baseball wasn't pulling fans into the parks anymore.

History has been kind to their effort, however. The ladies of the League indelibly left their mark on the game, a fact recognized by their enshrinement at Cooperstown, New York, a few years back. They're all there in the hallowed ground of the baseball Hall of Fame.

"It was something," Mary says, again with the modest voice that almost defies the achievement. "To walk in there with all those great ballplayers...to be inducted in our own place...it was something, well, something very, very special." The simple words are halted by a breath and a lump in her throat. An achievement recognized, a history appreciated, and an accomplishment immortalized can easily do that to a person.

While her professional career ended abruptly, her love of the game did not. Mary's still out there on the field today. She's not getting paid to pitch for her women's team, but they do have a sponsor to pick up the cost of their jerseys.

The ankle has healed, the spirit of competition never was dulled, and once again the fellowship of the basepaths is a part of Mary Moore's life in the game she has loved so well.

It's been a remarkable journey, all in all. She's rubbed elbows with the stars, she even has her own baseball card, and to top it off, she's a genuine baseball Hall of Famer. Not bad for a kid from Lincoln Park who dared to play a man's game, and who, incidentally, can still toss a pretty mean fastball when she's back there on the mound.

Does she miss the glory days? "Yeah, you bet I miss it. It was a lot of fun...a lot of good years."

No lump this time, but still too modestly recalled.

Forgotten,
But Not Gone

B eyond a patch of withering thistles and a locked gate is all that remains of the vessel *Columbia*.

Yards of rotting canvas flap hopelessly in the season's wind. A hundred, maybe a thousand orange life jackets are littered across the wooden dance floor where now only the feet of a dozen pigeons sway to the rhythm of the river's constant swells.

She floats on a sea of sadness, surrounded by the hissing sound of compressed air which emanates from the factory that co-joins her to the sagging dock. The silence of *Columbia* is deafening. She is dying, painfully. Deck by deck, season by season, hour by hour we lose her. She was the pride of the Detroit River when she was born over one hundred years ago. Now, she has little left but a good name and an unsullied reputation.

"She was built to be a boat of reputation," says the man who would be her caretaker and savior. "She was of quality throughout. Everything was first class on the *Columbia*, even down to the painted murals on the walls." He points to the sorry remains of murals that are now largely obscured by coats of carelessly applied paint that peels away in grotesque patches.

Bill Worden is a man in love with a mistress named *Columbia*. She was a river goddess who once reigned over an island named Bois Blanc, where her children came to make merry, to dance a night away, perhaps to fall in love, but always to quilt a patchwork of pleasant moments into a tapestry of lifetime memories. Now she is just an aging, benevolent queen, driven from her throne, exiled, abandoned, and simply dumped on her shores to die.

"That's why it's so important to try and save her," Bill Worden almost pleads. "She's one of only two of these great vessels left in existence. There just are no more of these anywhere in the world."

While she is clearly the victim of acute exposure to the elements, *Columbia* is still pure and strong. She was made of sturdy stuff back in 1902, so her heart is ready to pump again. If Bill Worden and the Steamer Columbia Foundation can interest a few more folks in another walk down her gangplank, a treasured jewel of the city's past may once again sound her thundering whistle in the beginnings of this new century.

Sadly, if the call to save *Columbia* is not answered, she'll be gone. She just can't take too many more nights of below-zero temperatures and summer days with nothing to do and no place to go. Her little sister, the *Ste. Claire*, was always clinging to *Columbia's* side, but she has now departed to what is hoped will be a renewed life in another place. So *Columbia* sits alone at the weakened dock these days, her future uncertain, but in the hands of those who know and love her best.

But at what cost could she sail again? What would it take to restore her? Is it even possible to make her seaworthy by today's maritime standards? Bill Worden has the rough figures and they are staggering.

"I think it'll take five or six million dollars to get her back." He says reluctantly. He's quick to add, "But she'd be the only one of her kind in the world." It's a tough sell, even for a committed preservationist.

While she's been away, *Columbia's* only destination has been taken from her. Bois Blanc, or what we knew as Bob-Lo Island, is gone forever. Instead of carousels and the giant Ferris wheel at its center, condominiums and golf courses for the wealthy have claimed the pathways and amusing spirit that brought so many to its shore.

For *Columbia*, perhaps there are other venues, other islands, other waters, in which she can seek dominion. Perhaps there are other memories for her to make, if there are those who wish to believe once again in the magic of the mistress of the moonlight.

Bill Worden believes it can happen. "I gotta tell you," he says with a different demeanor this time. "Wherever I go, whoever I tell about *Columbia*, it brings a smile to their faces. Everybody has a memory about standing on her bow, or staring at the river's swirls from her stern. I remember the great local bands, the dances, and all those dancers out there on the waxed floor..."